FOUNDATIONS OF AMERICAN
DEMOCRACY

FOUNDATIONS OF AMERICAN DEMOCRACY

A Critical Documents Reader

EDITED BY

W. Fitzhugh Brundage, Kathleen DuVal, Joseph T. Glatthaar, Sophia Howells, and Miguel La Serna

University of North Carolina at Chapel Hill DEPARTMENT OF HISTORY

This publication was supported by the College of Arts & Sciences at the University of North Carolina at Chapel Hill.

Copyright © 2025 by the University of North Carolina at Chapel Hill Department of History. All rights reserved.

ISBN 978-1-4696-8923-4 (paperback)
ISBN 978-1-4696-8924-1 (EPUB ebook)
ISBN 978-1-4696-9174-9 (PDF ebook)

Cover design by Ashley Muehlbauer

Published by the University of North Carolina at Chapel Hill Department of History

Distributed by the University of North Carolina Press

Table of Contents

Acknowledgments vii

Introduction, W. Fitzhugh Brundage, Kathleen DuVal, Joseph T. Glatthaar, Sophia Howells, and Miguel La Serna 1

I FOUNDATIONS 5

1. Declaration of Independence (1776)—Thomas Jefferson 7
   INTRODUCTION BY KATHLEEN DUVAL

2. Constitution of North Carolina (1776)—North Carolina Provincial Congress 13
   INTRODUCTION BY KATHLEEN DUVAL

3. Virginia Statute for Religious Freedom (1786)—Thomas Jefferson 23
   INTRODUCTION BY MOLLY WORTHEN

4. The Federalist Papers (1787)—James Madison, Alexander Hamilton 29
   INTRODUCTION BY MOLLY WORTHEN

5. The Federal Constitution (1789)—The Constitutional Convention 61
   INTRODUCTION BY W. FITZHUGH BRUNDAGE

II A MORE PERFECT UNION 87

6. Gettysburg Address (1863)—Abraham Lincoln 89
   INTRODUCTION BY JOSEPH T. GLATTHAAR

7. Abraham Lincoln's Second Inaugural Address (1865)—Abraham Lincoln 93
   INTRODUCTION BY W. FITZHUGH BRUNDAGE

8. Lecture Delivered at Franklin Hall (1832)—Maria W. Stewart 99
   INTRODUCTION BY KATHERINE TURK

9. What to the Slave is the Fourth of July? (1852)—Frederick Douglass 107
   INTRODUCTION BY ANTWAIN K. HUNTER

10   Emancipation Proclamation (1862)—Abraham Lincoln 115
INTRODUCTION BY JOSEPH T. GLATTHAAR

11   The Fourteenth Amendment (1868)—John A. Bingham and others 121
INTRODUCTION BY W. FITZHUGH BRUNDAGE

12   Testimony on the Ku Klux Klan in North Carolina (1871) —Joseph G. Hester 127
INTRODUCTION BY ANTWAIN K. HUNTER

III THE GOSPEL OF FREEDOM 137

13   Chinese Exclusion Act (1882)—United States Congress 139
INTRODUCTION BY HEATHER RUTH LEE

14   The Indian's Plea for Freedom (1919)—Charles A. Eastman (Ohiyesa) 147
INTRODUCTION BY RAQUEL ESCOBAR

15   Four Freedoms (1941)—Franklin D. Roosevelt 153
INTRODUCTION BY ERIK S. GELLMAN

16   Executive Order 9066 (1942)—Franklin D. Roosevelt 161
INTRODUCTION BY HEATHER RUTH LEE

17   Mendez v. Westminster (1946)—Paul J. McCormick 167
INTRODUCTION BY RAQUEL ESCOBAR

18   To Secure These Rights (1947)—The President's Committee on Civil Rights 177
INTRODUCTION BY ERIK S. GELLMAN

19   Brown v. Board of Education of Topeka (1954)—Earl Warren 187
INTRODUCTION BY ANTWAIN K. HUNTER

20   Letter from the Birmingham Jail (1963)—Martin Luther King Jr. 195
INTRODUCTION BY CLAUDE A. CLEGG

21   Equal Rights Amendment (1972)—Alice Paul and Crystal Eastman 199
INTRODUCTION BY KATHERINE TURK

Contributors 203

Acknowledgments

This volume is a testament to collective effort and collegiality at all levels. The endeavor would not be possible without the support of James W. C. White, Craver Family Dean of the College of Arts and Sciences at the University of North Carolina at Chapel Hill (UNC-CH), and Noreen McDonald, Senior Associate Dean for Social Sciences and Global Programs in the UNC-CH College of Arts and Science. We are grateful for the financial support of the College of Arts and Sciences that allowed this project to come to fruition. We thank Nathan Knuffman, UNC-CH Vice Chancellor for Finance & Operations, for supporting the Department of History's collaboration with the University of North Carolina Press.

This work was a true collaboration of faculty, staff, and students in the UNC-CH Department of History. We are grateful to each of the faculty contributors, W. Fitzhugh Brundage, Claude A. Clegg, Kathleen DuVal, Raquel Escobar, Joseph T. Glatthaar, Erik S. Gellman, Antwain K. Hunter, Heather Ruth Lee, Katherine Turk, and Molly Worthen, for preparing each chapter in this volume with such care, insight, and industriousness. Our history work-study undergraduates were all-hands-on-deck when it came to proofreading, copyediting, and collating the material that went into the volume. To this end, we are immensely grateful for the contributions of Daniela Marin-Lopez, Luke Lambeth, and Jacob Schwier. We are indebted to the talented Lab At UNC-CH (LAUNCH) graduate student directors, Dani Mcivor and Nicholas Sifford, who formatted this document's imagery, and to faculty director Lauren Jarvis for her support and supervision. Similarly, we thank our incredible staff—Caleb Brimmer, Shakierah Clark, Sophia Howells, Sam Louie-Meadors, and Jonathan Woody—for supporting us every possible way, every step of the way. Any department is only ever as good as its staff, and we are fortunate to have the best staff in the business.

We are humbled by the enthusiastic support we received from the University of North Carolina Press. Debbie Gershenowitz recognized the potential and appeal of an American democracy reader right away and championed the project from the moment of its inception. Sam Dalzell provided patient guidance throughout the process, and the creative and production teams at UNC Press worked wonders with the manuscript in record time. We owe a tremendous debt of gratitude to UNC Press Chief Operating Officer and Director of the Office of Scholarly Publishing Services, John McLeod. John's vision, patience, and creativity at every stage of the process were instrumental in bringing the volume from a mere concept to a book of pedagogical and scholarly value. Rare are the times when a chief operating officer takes such an active and constructive role in a book project, and this book is all the better for it.

Finally, we thank the students, staff, faculty, emerita, and alumni of the UNC-CH Department of History for providing the intellectual and collaborative environment that allows endeavors like this one to take root and flourish. We dedicate this work to this collegial community of historians.

FOUNDATIONS OF AMERICAN DEMOCRACY

Introduction

In *Federalist Paper* No. 51, James Madison reflected on the purpose of government. "If men were angels," he wrote, "no government would be necessary." But the leaders of the American Revolution and the framers of the U.S. Constitution knew they lived in the real world and were tasked with "framing a government which is to be administered by men over men." Madison acknowledged, "The great difficulty lies in this: you must first enable the government to control the governed; and in the next place oblige it to control itself." The proper balance between order and liberty—having a system that effectively governs without becoming tyrannical and that requires people to sacrifice some rights in order to protect more cherished rights—was the central concern of the founders. Madison and the Constitution's other framers built checks and balances into the governmental structure that they designed. But they also knew that, as Madison put it, "the primary control on the government" had to be "the people."[1]

The questions at the heart of the founding of the American republic have been central throughout the nation's history. Who are "the people," and how do they make their wills known? How do the people balance liberty and order without tipping into either anarchy or tyranny? Who should represent the people, and how much should they be beholden to our will? Is it possible for government, in the words of the Constitution's Preamble, to "secure the Blessings of Liberty to ourselves and our Posterity"?[2]

Reading the founding documents of the United States, understanding them in their historical context, and tracing the 250 years of progress and challenges in the evolution of democratic republicanism in America and the effort to form "a more perfect Union" can help us answer essential questions about governance and democracy. Those are vital questions for our present and for the next 250 years of this country. Applying fundamental questions of American democracy to important texts of the past is the purpose of this volume.

The book is broken into three parts. Part One, *Foundations*, offers a selection of critical documents that laid the groundwork on which the American experiment was built. We begin with the Declaration of

Independence. In July 1776, the Continental Congress asserted that the purpose of government was to protect the people's right to "Life, Liberty and the pursuit of Happiness." British governance over the colonies had become, they declared to the world, "destructive of these ends," and it was the people's right "to institute new Government, laying its foundation on such principles and organizing its powers in such form, as to them shall seem most likely to effect their Safety and Happiness."[3] That same year, the states began writing their own state constitutions to create new governmental structures there. Although less well known than the U.S. Constitution, the constitutions of North Carolina and the other states in most cases had more day-to-day effects on people and created many of the protections that eventually were added to the U.S. Constitution in the Bill of Rights.

Part Two, *A More Perfect Union*, offers a selection of documents related to the American Civil War and Reconstruction. Since the Missouri Crisis of 1818–1820, the Free and Slave States struggled over control of the territories and the future direction of the country. This conflict destroyed every major intersectional institution in the United States and, eventually, the nation itself. Eleven states sought to overturn the outcome of a free and fair election by seceding from the United States. Those remaining states viewed the Constitution as the bedrock of political freedom and economic advancement. Liberty and economic success went hand-in-hand, and secession threatened those blessings. The implacable differences prompted both sections to resort to arms. As the war dragged on, the Union came to grips with the underlying cause of the war, slavery, by issuing the Emancipation Proclamation, and not long after the Union won, it adopted the Thirteenth Amendment abolishing slavery. Yet that did not determine what rights newfound freedom offered. Throughout the period of Reconstruction and in the years afterward, Black men and women eagerly sought equal rights with whites, yet many white people in both the South and the North resisted those efforts, sometimes resorting to violence.

Part Three, *The Gospel of Freedom*, highlights the challenges and struggles of generations of Americans who demanded participation and representation in American democracy. In his 1963 "Letter from a Birmingham Jail," Reverend Martin Luther King Jr. wrote, "We know through painful experience that freedom is never voluntarily given by the oppressor; it must be demanded by the oppressed."[4] The documents in Part Three are a testament to King's words, highlighting the different ways that ordinary women and men have challenged, defined, and redefined citizenship in the long struggle for Civil Rights.

The documents collated here tell many stories, and they also provide insights into three key features of American democracy. First, it is imperfect. Try as they did to anticipate problems and contradictions that would emerge as the young nation grew and evolved, American nation-makers were limited by their own position in society and its preferences and prejudices, their own blind spots, and their own historical context. As a result, the founding documents left large groups of people—women, the working classes, people of color—out of their authors' conceptualizations of a free republic. A "perfect" union has never existed in the United States. Rather, it is the goal of building a union "more perfect" than it currently is that has united so many generations of Americans. Second, American democracy is a process. The founding documents analyzed in Part One should be viewed not as definitive end points but rather as the beginning of a larger conversation about what this nation is and ought to be. As with all foundations, these documents laid the groundwork upon which American democracy has been, and continues to be, built. Parts Two and Three highlight the different ways that this process has unfolded throughout America's history. That process has been messy, complex, and unequally distributed; it is also incomplete. Finally, American democracy is negotiated. Throughout the course of U.S. history, people from all walks of life have asserted their right to have rights, to participate in the democratic process, to be seen, to be heard. Part Three offers a glimpse into some of these struggles and to the structural, legal, linguistic, and cultural barriers that everyday women, men, workers, immigrants, and people of color have faced in order to carve out a space for themselves in American society.

Jefferson's insistence that government is intended for our "safety and happiness" might sound naïve or antiquated. Yet the words of those who have gone before remind us that Americans have sacrificed and died to defend and advance American democracy. Perhaps, with Abraham Lincoln, we might decide "that these dead shall not have died in vain" and renew our resolve "that government of the people, by the people, for the people, shall not perish from the earth."[5]—W. Fitzhugh Brundage, Kathleen DuVal, Joseph T. Glatthaar, Sophia Howells, and Miguel La Serna

Notes

[1] James Madison, *Federalist* No. 51, in this volume.
[2] U.S. Constitution, preamble, in this volume.
[3] Declaration of Independence, in this volume.
[4] Martin Luther King Jr., Letter from Birmingham Jail, available from outside sources.
[5] Declaration of Independence and Gettysburg Address, both in this volume.

PART ONE

FOUNDATIONS

The first printing of the Declaration of Independence, printed on July 4, 1776 by John Dunlap, a Philadelphia printer. (Library of Congress)

1

Declaration of Independence (1776)

Thomas Jefferson

Introduction

At the start of 1776, few colonists imagined that their protests would lead to independence. Shots had been fired the previous April at Lexington and Concord, in Massachusetts, so when the Second Continental Congress assembled in Philadelphia in May 1775, its delegates voted to create a Continental Army. But in July 1775, in what became known as the Olive Branch Petition, the delegates to Congress were still calling themselves "your Majesty's faithful subjects" and asking the King to intervene to prevent Parliament's tyranny over the colonies.

It was not until Thomas Paine in January 1776 published *Common Sense* that public opinion significantly shifted toward believing that an independent country without a king was not a crazy idea—it was "common sense." Before *Common Sense*, no colony had instructed its delegates to vote for independence, and three had sent them to Philadelphia specifically forbidding them from doing so. But on April 12, North Carolina's Provincial Assembly, meeting at Halifax, became the first to tell its delegates that they could vote for independence, in what became known as the Halifax Resolves.

In Congress on June 7, 1776, Virginia delegate Richard Henry Lee proposed a resolution declaring American independence. Congress selected a committee to write a declaration of independence that would explain colonists' reasons for separating from the British empire. Virginia delegate Thomas Jefferson drafted the declaration, and fellow committee members John Adams and Benjamin Franklin edited it before the committee presented it to Congress.

In previous petitions, Congress had blamed Parliament for the troubles. Jefferson's Declaration of Independence, though, charged King George III with a series of betrayals of his responsibility to the colonies. Congress deleted Jefferson's accusation that King George III had forced slavery on the colonists but approved of most of the draft. Congress voted for independence on July 2 and approved and signed the final version of the declaration on July 4. Two hundred copies immediately were printed to be circulated through the rebelling colonies.

Throughout the centuries since 1776, people have used Jefferson's ringing declaration that "all men are created equal" as an inspiration and a call for equality and freedom, from the French and Haitian revolutions to today.— Kathleen DuVal

The unanimous Declaration of the thirteen united States of America, When in the Course of human events, it becomes necessary for one people to dissolve the political bands which have connected them with another, and to assume among the powers of the earth, the separate and equal station to which the Laws of Nature and of Nature's God entitle them, a decent respect to the opinions of mankind requires that they should declare the causes which impel them to the separation.

We hold these truths to be self-evident, that all men are created equal, that they are endowed by their Creator with certain unalienable Rights, that among these are Life, Liberty and the pursuit of Happiness.—That to secure these rights, Governments are instituted among Men, deriving their just powers from the consent of the governed,—That whenever any Form of Government becomes destructive of these ends, it is the Right of the People to alter or to abolish it, and to institute new Government, laying its foundation on such principles and organizing its powers in such form, as to them shall seem most likely to effect their Safety and Happiness. Prudence, indeed, will dictate that Governments long established should not be changed for light and transient causes; and accordingly all experience hath shewn, that mankind are more disposed to suffer, while evils are sufferable, than to right themselves by abolishing the forms to which they are accustomed. But when a long train of abuses and usurpations, pursuing invariably the same Object evinces a design to reduce them under absolute Despotism, it is their right, it is their duty, to throw off such Government, and to provide new Guards for their future security. —Such has been the patient sufferance of these Colonies; and such is now the necessity which constrains them to alter their former Systems of Government. The history of the present King of Great Britain is a history of repeated injuries and usurpations, all having in direct object the establishment of an absolute

Tyranny over these States. To prove this, let Facts be submitted to a candid world.

He has refused his Assent to Laws, the most wholesome and necessary for the public good.

He has forbidden his Governors to pass Laws of immediate and pressing importance, unless suspended in their operation till his Assent should be obtained; and when so suspended, he has utterly neglected to attend to them.

He has refused to pass other Laws for the accommodation of large districts of people, unless those people would relinquish the right of Representation in the Legislature, a right inestimable to them and formidable to tyrants only.

He has called together legislative bodies at places unusual, uncomfortable, and distant from the depository of their public Records, for the sole purpose of fatiguing them into compliance with his measures.

He has dissolved Representative Houses repeatedly, for opposing with manly firmness his invasions on the rights of the people.

He has refused for a long time, after such dissolutions, to cause others to be elected; whereby the Legislative powers, incapable of Annihilation, have returned to the People at large for their exercise; the State remaining in the mean time exposed to all the dangers of invasion from without, and convulsions within.

He has endeavoured to prevent the population of these States; for that purpose obstructing the Laws for Naturalization of Foreigners; refusing to pass others to encourage their migrations hither, and raising the conditions of new Appropriations of Lands.

He has obstructed the Administration of Justice, by refusing his Assent to Laws for establishing Judiciary powers.

He has made Judges dependent on his Will alone, for the tenure of their offices, and the amount and payment of their salaries.

He has erected a multitude of New Offices, and sent hither swarms of Officers to harrass our people, and eat out their substance.

He has kept among us, in times of peace, Standing Armies without the Consent of our legislatures.

He has affected to render the Military independent of and superior to the Civil power.

He has combined with others to subject us to a jurisdiction foreign to our constitution, and unacknowledged by our laws; giving his Assent to their Acts of pretended Legislation:

For Quartering large bodies of armed troops among us:

For protecting them, by a mock Trial, from punishment for any Murders which they should commit on the Inhabitants of these States:

For cutting off our Trade with all parts of the world:

For imposing Taxes on us without our Consent:

For depriving us in many cases, of the benefits of Trial by Jury:

For transporting us beyond Seas to be tried for pretended offences:

For abolishing the free System of English Laws in a neighbouring Province, establishing therein an Arbitrary government, and enlarging its Boundaries so as to render it at once an example and fit instrument for introducing the same absolute rule into these Colonies:

For taking away our Charters, abolishing our most valuable Laws, and altering fundamentally the Forms of our Governments:

For suspending our own Legislatures, and declaring themselves invested with power to legislate for us in all cases whatsoever.

He has abdicated Government here, by declaring us out of his Protection and waging War against us.

He has plundered our seas, ravaged our Coasts, burnt our towns, and destroyed the lives of our people.

He is at this time transporting large Armies of foreign Mercenaries to compleat the works of death, desolation and tyranny, already begun with circumstances of Cruelty & perfidy scarcely paralleled in the most barbarous ages, and totally unworthy the Head of a civilized nation.

He has constrained our fellow Citizens taken Captive on the high Seas to bear Arms against their Country, to become the executioners of their friends and Brethren, or to fall themselves by their Hands.

He has excited domestic insurrections amongst us, and has endeavoured to bring on the inhabitants of our frontiers, the merciless Indian Savages, whose known rule of warfare, is an undistinguished destruction of all ages, sexes and conditions.

In every stage of these Oppressions We have Petitioned for Redress in the most humble terms: Our repeated Petitions have been answered only by repeated injury. A Prince whose character is thus marked by every act which may define a Tyrant, is unfit to be the ruler of a free people.

Nor have We been wanting in attentions to our Brittish brethren. We have warned them from time to time of attempts by their legislature to extend an unwarrantable jurisdiction over us. We have reminded them of the circumstances of our emigration and settlement here. We have appealed to their native justice and magnanimity, and we have conjured them by the ties of our common kindred to disavow these usurpations, which, would inevitably interrupt our connections and correspondence. They too have been deaf to the voice of justice and of consanguinity. We must, therefore, acquiesce in the necessity, which denounces our Separation, and hold them, as we hold the rest of mankind, Enemies in War, in Peace Friends.

We, therefore, the Representatives of the united States of America, in General Congress, Assembled, appealing to the Supreme Judge of the world for the rectitude of our intentions, do, in the Name, and by Authority of the good People of these Colonies, solemnly publish and declare, That these United Colonies are, and of Right ought to be Free and Independent States; that they are Absolved from all Allegiance to the British Crown, and that all political connection between them and the State of Great Britain, is and ought to be totally dissolved; and that as Free and Independent States, they have full Power to levy War, conclude Peace, contract Alliances, establish Commerce, and to do all other Acts and Things which Independent States may of right do. And for the support of this Declaration, with a firm reliance on the protection of divine Providence, we mutually pledge to each other our Lives, our Fortunes and our sacred Honor.

Questions for Discussion

1. What do the Declaration's first two paragraphs lay out as the reasons for separating from Britain?
2. According to the Declaration of Independence, why do governments exist?
3. Choose one charge against King George III and explain it.
4. Do you think the Declaration's reasons for rebellion were enough justification for colonists to feel that "it is their right, it is their duty, to throw off [the British] Government"?

Further Reading

Continental Congress. The Articles of Confederation. 1777. https://www.archives.gov/milestone-documents/articles-of-confederation

Continental Congress. Olive Branch Petition. 1775. https://founders.archives.gov/documents/Jefferson/01-01-02-0114

North Carolina Provincial Congress. Halifax Resolves. 1776. https://www.carolana.com/NC/Documents/nc_halifax_resolves.html

Paine, Thomas. *Common Sense*. 1776. https://americainclass.org/thomas-paine-common-sense-1776

THE
CONSTITUTION,
OR
FORM OF GOVERNMENT,

AGREED TO, AND RESOLVED UPON,

BY THE

REPRESENTATIVES of the FREEMEN

OF THE

STATE

OF

NORTH-CAROLINA,

ELECTED and CHOSEN for that particular PURPOSE,

IN CONGRESS ASSEMBLED, AT HALIFAX,

The Eighteenth Day of *December*, in the Year of our LORD
One Thousand Seven Hundred and Seventy-Six.

PHILADELPHIA:
PRINTED BY F. BAILEY, IN MARKET-STREET.
M.DCC.LXXIX.

The 1868 North Carolina State Constitution, the state's second constitution, adopted after the Civil War. (*Documenting the American South*, UNC-Chapel Hill Libraries)

2

Constitution of North Carolina (1776)

North Carolina Provincial Congress

Introduction

Once the Continental Congress declared American independence, the thirteen rebelling colonies—now states—needed their own state constitutions to establish and legitimize their new governing structures. Many of the men who gathered in Halifax late in 1776 had been elected to North Carolina's colonial assembly before the Revolution. As the Revolution began, they held a series of Provincial Congresses. The state constitution was written by the final Provincial Congress. Richard Caswell of New Bern served as its president and was chosen as the state's first governor under the provisions of this state constitution.

The framers of North Carolina's first state constitution were tasked with adapting what they admired from the British political system to the conditions of American independence. Some of the state constitutions, including North Carolina's, were more democratic than either the British system or the eventual U.S. Constitution.

North Carolina's constitution has changed since 1776. In 1835, a state convention wrote amendments that made major changes to the constitution, including increasing the size of both branches of the legislature. In 1868, when North Carolina re-entered the Union after seceding during the Civil War, the state adopted an entirely new state constitution. That constitution abolished slavery and expanded voting rights. By 1971, so many amendments had clogged the 1868 constitution—including ones restricting voting rights—that a new convention substantially revised the constitution, creating the one in place today.

The 1776 North Carolina constitution has two parts: a declaration of rights and provisions laying out the form of the state's government.
—Kathleen DuVal

A Declaration of Rights, &c.

   I. That all political power is vested in and derived from the people only.
  II. That the people of this State ought to have the sole and exclusive right of regulating the internal government and police thereof.
 III. That no man or set of men are entitled to exclusive or separate emoluments or privileges from the community, but in consideration of public services.
  IV. That the legislative, executive, and supreme judicial powers of government, ought to be forever separate and distinct from each other.
   V. That all powers of suspending laws, or the execution of laws, by any authority, without consent of the Representatives of the people, is injurious to their rights, and ought not to be exercised.
  VI. That elections of members, to serve as Representatives in General Assembly, ought to be free.
 VII. That, in all criminal prosecutions, every man has a right to be informed of the accusation against him, and to confront the accusers and witnesses with other testimony, and shall not be compelled to give evidence against himself.
VIII. That no freeman shall be put to answer any criminal charge, but by indictment, presentment, or impeachment.
  IX. That no freeman shall be convicted of any crime, but by the unanimous verdict of a jury of good and lawful men, in open court, as heretofore used.
   X. That excessive bail should not be required, nor excessive fines imposed, nor cruel or unusual punishments inflicted.
  XI. That general warrants—whereby an officer or messenger may he commanded to search suspected places, without evidence of the fact committed, or to seize any person or persons, not named, whose offences are not particularly described, and supported by evidence—are dangerous to liberty, and ought not to be granted.
 XII. That no freeman ought to be taken, imprisoned, or disseized of his freehold liberties or privileges, or outlawed, or exiled,

or in any manner destroyed, or deprived of his life, liberty, or property, but by the law of the land.

XIII. That every freeman, restrained of his liberty, is entitled to a remedy, to inquire into the lawfulness thereof, and to remove the same, if unlawful; and that such remedy ought not to be denied or delayed.

XIV. That in all controversies at law, respecting property, the ancient mode of trial, by jury, is one of the best securities of the rights of the people, and ought to remain sacred and inviolable.

XV. That the freedom of the press is one of the great bulwarks of liberty, and therefore ought never to be restrained.

XVI. That the people of this State ought not to be taxed, or made subject to the payment of any impost or duty, without the consent of themselves, or their Representatives in General Assembly, freely given.

XVII. That the people have a right to bear arms, for the defence of the State; and, as standing armies, in time of peace, are dangerous to liberty, they ought not to be kept up; and that the military should be kept under strict subordination to, and governed by, the civil power.

XVIII. That the people have a right to assemble together, to consult for their common good, to instruct their Representatives, and to apply to the Legislature, for redress of grievances.

XIX. That all men have a natural and unalienable right to worship Almighty God according to the dictates of their own consciences.

XX. That, for redress of grievances, and for amending and strengthening the laws, elections ought to be often held.

XXI. That a frequent recurrence to fundamental principles is absolutely necessary, to preserve the blessings of liberty.

XXII. That no hereditary emoluments, privileges or honors ought to be granted or conferred in this State.

XXIII. That perpetuities and monopolies are contrary to the genius of a free State, and ought not to be allowed.

XXIV. That retrospective laws, punishing facts committed before the existence of such laws, and by them only declared criminal, are oppressive, unjust, and incompatible with liberty; wherefore no ex post facto law ought to be made.

XXV. The property of the soil, in a free government, being one of the essential rights of the collective body of the people, it is necessary, in order to avoid future disputes, that the limits of the State should be ascertained with precision. [Here the text describes North Carolina's southern and northern borders.] Provided always, That this Declaration of Rights shall not prejudice any nation or nations of Indians, from enjoying such hunting-grounds as may have been, or hereafter shall be, secured to them by any former or future Legislature of this State:—And provided also, That it shall not be construed so as to prevent the establishment of one or more governments westward of this State, by consent of the Legislature:—And provided further, That nothing herein contained shall affect the titles or repossessions of individuals holding or claiming under the laws heretofore in force, or grants heretofore made by the late King George the Second, or his predecessors, or the late lords proprietors, or any of them.

The Constitution, or Form of Government, &c

WHEREAS Allegiance and Protection are in their nature reciprocal, and the one should of right be refused, when the other is withdrawn,

And whereas George the third King of Great Britain, and late Sovereign of the British American Colonies, hath not only withdrawn from them his Protection, but by an Act of the British Legislature, declared the Inhabitants of these States out of the Protection of the British Crown and all their property found upon the high Seas, liable to be seized and Confiscated to the uses mentioned in the said Act, And the said George the Third has also sent Fleets and Armies to prosecute a cruel war against them for the purpose of reducing the Inhabitants of the said Colonies to a State of Abject Slavery. In Consequence whereof all Government under the said King within the said Colonies hath ceased and a Total Dissolution of Government in many of them hath taken place;

And whereas the Continental Congress having considered the Premises and other previous Violations of the rights of the good People of America have therefore Declared that the thirteen United Colonies are of right wholly absolved from all Allegiance to the British Crown or any other Foreign Jurisdiction whatsoever and that the said Colonies now are and forever shall be free and Independent States.

Wherefore in our present State in Order to prevent Anarchy and Confusion, it becomes necessary that a Government should be established in this State. Therefore we the Representatives of the Freemen of North Carolina chosen and Assembled in Congress for the Express purpose of framing a Constitution under the Authority of the People most Conducive to their Happiness and Prosperity do declare that a Government for this State shall be established in manner and form following, to wit.

I. That the Legislative Authority shall be vested in two Distinct Branches, both dependent on the People, to wit, a Senate and house of Commons.
II. That the Senate shall be composed of Representatives annually chosen by Ballot, one for each county in the State.
III. That the house of Commons shall be composed of Representatives annually chosen by Ballot, two for each County and one for each of the Towns of Edenton, New Bern, Wilmington, Salisbury, Hillsborough and Halifax. . . .
V. That each Member of the Senate shall have usually resided in the County in which he is chosen, for one year immediately preceding his Election and for the same time shall have possessed and continue to possess in the County which he represents not less than three hundred Acres of Land in Fee.
VI. That each Member of the house of Commons shall have usually resided in the County in which he is chosen for one year immediately preceding his Election and for six months shall have possessed and continue to possess in the County which he represents not less than one hundred Acres of Land in Fee or for the Term of his own Life.
VII. That all Freemen of the Age of twenty-one Years who have been Inhabitants of any one County within the State twelve months immediately preceding the Day of any Election and possessed of a Freehold within the same County of Fifty Acres of Land for six months next before and at the day of Election shall be entitled to Vote for a Member of the Senate.
VIII. That all Freemen of the Age of twenty-one Years, who have been Inhabitants of any County within this State twelve months immediately preceding the day of any Election and shall have paid Public Taxes, shall be entitled to Vote for

Members of the house of Commons for the County in which he resides. . . .

XIII. That the General Assembly shall by joint Ballot of both Houses appoint Judges of the Supreme Courts of Law and Equity, Judges of Admiralty, and Attorney General who shall be commissioned by the Governor and hold their Offices during good behavior.

XIV. That the Senate and House of Commons shall have Power to appoint the Generals and Field-Officers of the Militia, and all Officers of the regular Army of this State.

XV. That the Senate and House of Commons, jointly at their first Meeting after each annual Election, shall by Ballot elect a Governor for one year, who shall not be eligible to that Office longer than three Years, in six successive Years. That no Person under thirty years of age, and who has not been a Resident in this State above five Years, and having in the State a Freehold in Lands and Tenements above the Value of one Thousand Pounds, shall be eligible as Governor.

XVI. That the Senate and House of Commons, jointly at their first Meeting after each annual Election, shall by Ballot elect seven persons to be a Council of State for one Year, who shall advise the Governor in the Execution of his Office. . . .

XVIII. That Governor, for the time being, shall be Captain-General and Commander in Chief of the Militia; and, in the Recess of the General Assembly, shall have Power, by and with the Advice of the Council of State, to embody the Militia for the public Safety.

XIX. That the Governor, for the time being, shall have Power to draw for and apply such Sums of Money as shall be voted by the General Assembly, for the Contingencies of Government, and be accountable to them for the same. He also may, by and with the Advice of the Council of State, lay Embargoes, or prohibit the Exportation of any Commodity, for any Term not exceeding thirty Days, at any one Time in the Recess of the General Assembly; and shall have the Power of granting Pardons and Reprieves, except where the Prosecution shall be carried on by the General Assembly, or the Law shall otherwise direct; in which Case he may in the Recess grant a

	Reprieve until the next Sitting of the General Assembly; And may exercise all the other executive Powers of Government, limited and restrained as by this Constitution is mentioned, and according to the Laws of the State....
XXI.	That the Governor, Judges of the Supreme Court of Law and Equity, Judges of Admiralty, and Attorney-General, shall have adequate Salaries during their Continuance in Office....
XXVII.	That no Officer in the regular Army or Navy, in the Service and Pay of the United States, of this or any other State, nor any Contractor or Agent for supplying such Army or Navy with Clothing or Provisions, shall have a Seat either in the Senate, House of Commons, or Council of State....
XXXI.	That no Clergyman, or Preacher of the Gospel of any Denomination, shall be capable of being a Member of either the Senate, House of Commons, or Council of State, while he continues in the exercise of the pastoral Function.
XXXII.	That no Person, who shall deny the being of God or the Truth of the Protestant Religion, or the Divine Authority either of the Old or New Testament, or who shall hold Religious Principles Incompatible with the Freedom and Safety of the State, shall be capable of holding any Office or Place of Trust or Profit in the Civil Department within this State....
XXXIV.	That there shall be no Establishment of any one Religious Church in this State, in Preference to any other; neither shall any Person, on any Pretence whatsoever, be compelled to attend any Place of Worship contrary to his own Faith or Judgment, nor be obliged to pay, for the Purchase of any Glebe, or the building of any House of Worship, or for the Maintenance of any Minister or Ministry, contrary to what he believes right, of has voluntarily and personally engaged to perform; but all Persons shall be at Liberty to exercise their own Mode of Worship: Provided, That nothing herein contained shall be construed to exempt Preachers of treasonable or seditious Discourses, from legal Trial and Punishment....
XXXVII.	That the Delegates for this State, to the Continental Congress while necessary, shall be chosen annually by the

General Assembly, by Ballot . . . and no Person shall be elected to serve in that Capacity for more than three Years successively. . . .

XXXIX. That the Person of a Debtor, where there is not a strong Presumption of Fraud, shall not be confined in Prison, after delivering up, bona fide, all his Estate real and personal, for the Use of his Creditors in such Manner as shall be hereafter regulated by Law. All Prisoners shall be bailable by sufficient Sureties, unless for capital Offences when the Proof is evident or the Presumption great.

XL. That every Foreigner, who comes to Settle in this State having first taken an Oath of Allegiance to the same, may purchase, or, by other just Means, acquire, hold, and transfer Land, or other real Estate; and after one year's residence, shall be deemed a Free Citizen.

XLI. That a School or Schools shall be established by the Legislature, for the convenient Instruction of Youth, with such Salaries to the Masters, paid by the Public, as may enable them to instruct at low Prices; and all useful Learning shall be duly encouraged, and promoted, in one or more Universities.

XLII. That no Purchase of Lands shall be made of the Indian Natives, but on Behalf of the Public, and by Authority of the General Assembly.

XLIII. That the future Legislature of this State shall regulate entails[1] in such a manner as to prevent Perpetuities. . . .

XLV. That any Member of either House of the General Assembly shall have Liberty to dissent from, and protest against any Act or Resolve, which he may think Injurious to the public, or any Individual, and have the Reasons of his Dissent entered on the Journals. . . .

Questions for Discussion

1. Why do you think the framers of the 1776 North Carolina state constitution decided to start it with a declaration of rights?

2. Who got to vote in North Carolina in 1776? Who did not?

3. Having read the Declaration of Independence, can you connect any of the charges that it makes against King George III to any of the protections provided by North Carolina's first state constitution?

Further Reading

Charter of Carolina. 1663. https://avalon.law.yale.edu/17th_century/nc01.asp
Constitution of the Cherokee Nation. 1827/ https://www.wcu.edu/library/DigitalCollections/CherokeePhoenix/Vol1/no01/constitution-of-the-cherokee-nation-page-1-column-2a-page-2-column-3a.html
Current North Carolina State Constitution. 1971. https://www.ncleg.gov/Laws/Constitution
Magna Carta. 1215. https://www.nationalarchives.gov.uk/education/resources/magna-carta/british-library-magna-carta-1215-runnymede/
North Carolina State Constitution of 1868/ https://docsouth.unc.edu/nc/conv1868/conv1868.html

Note

1. An entail was a legal restriction that kept property and wealth within a certain family line.

This official presidential portrait of Thomas Jefferson was painted in 1800 by Rembrandt Peale. (Library of Congress)

3

Virginia Statute for Religious Freedom (1786)

Thomas Jefferson

Introduction

After the revolution, American clergy and politicians faced an unprecedented problem: how to order the relationship between organized religion and civil government in a brand-new country with unparalleled religious pluralism, full of citizens with a deep suspicion of any arrangement that too closely resembled the Church of England's privileged place in Britain. Prior to independence, each colony had managed this challenge differently. Several, such as Connecticut, Massachusetts, and Virginia, supported an established church—that is, one Protestant denomination that received tax funds and other privileges. Others, like Rhode Island and Pennsylvania, did not.

The debate over church establishment in Virginia set the stage for the national conversation. Thomas Jefferson, who became governor in 1779, worked with religious dissenters to advocate for a future with no official state church. Baptists, for example, shared his opposition to granting special privileges to any single denomination. (Before the war, the colonial government in Virginia had supported the Church of England.) Jefferson himself rejected many Christian doctrines; he and the Baptists approached the issue from different perspectives. But both felt that religious belief was an individual choice, and the government shouldn't interfere. Some Founding Fathers argued instead that the government should divide up its support among several different churches and create multiple establishments. And almost everyone thought of America as a broadly Protestant country. (In New York, John Jay tried unsuccessfully to convince his colleagues to ban Catholics from holding office.) But more and more Virginians concluded that if the government picked favorites between religious institutions, tyranny would result.

In 1786, the Virginia legislature passed the bill that Jefferson wrote "for establishing religious freedom." The law outlawed government aid to all religious groups and guaranteed freedom of worship to all, not just to Protestants. The words printed in italics were later deleted by Senate amendment, but we reproduce them here to show how the text of the bill evolved over the course of the debate—especially in the bill's preamble, which lays out an interesting argument about how best to pursue truth and nurture a free and virtuous community.

The Virginia law influenced debates in other states although Connecticut and Massachusetts continued to support the established Congregational church until 1818 and 1833, respectively. Even today in North Carolina, the state constitution bans from public office "any person who shall deny the being of Almighty God." The Supreme Court banned religious tests for office in 1961, rendering this clause void, but it reveals the remnants of established religion today.— Molly Worthen

A Bill for Establishing Religious Freedom
Drafted by Thomas Jefferson
Passed by the Virginia General Assembly on January 16, 1786

Well aware that the opinions and belief of men depend not on their own will, but follow involuntarily the evidence proposed to their minds; that Almighty God hath created the mind free, and manifested his supreme will that free it shall remain by making it altogether insusceptible of restraint; that all attempts to influence it by temporal punishments, or burthens, or by civil incapacitations, tend only to beget habits of hypocrisy and meanness, and are a departure from the plan of the holy author of our religion, who being lord both of body and mind, yet chose not to propagate it by coercions on either, as was in his Almighty power to do, *but to extend it by its influence on reason alone;* that the impious presumption of legislators and rulers, civil as well as ecclesiastical, who, being themselves but fallible and uninspired men, have assumed dominion over the faith of others, setting up their own opinions and modes of thinking as the only true and infallible, and as such endeavoring to impose them on others, hath established and maintained false religions over the greatest part of the world and through all time: That to compel a man to furnish contributions of money for the propagation of opinions which he disbelieves *and abhors,* is sinful and tyrannical; that even the forcing him to support this or that teacher of his own religious persuasion, is depriving him of the comfortable liberty of giving his contributions to the particular pastor whose morals he would make his pattern, and whose powers he feels most persuasive to righteousness; and is withdrawing from the ministry those temporary rewards, which proceeding from an approbation of their personal conduct, are an additional incitement to earnest and unremitting labours for the instruction of mankind; that our civil rights have no dependance on our religious opinions, any more than our opinions in physics or geometry; that therefore the proscribing any citizen as unworthy the public confidence by laying upon him an incapacity of being called to offices of trust and emolument, unless he profess or renounce this or that religious opinion, is depriving him injuriously of those privileges and advantages to which, in common with his fellow citizens, he has a natural right; that it tends also to corrupt the principles of that *very* religion it is meant to encourage, by bribing, with a monopoly of worldly honours and emoluments, those who will externally profess and conform to it; that though indeed these are criminal who do not withstand such temptation, yet neither are those innocent who lay the bait in their way; *that the opinions of men are not the object of civil government, nor under its jurisdiction;* that to suffer the civil magistrate to intrude his powers into the field of opinion and to restrain the profession or propagation of principles on supposition of their ill tendency is a dangerous fallacy, which at once destroys all religious liberty, because he being of course judge of that tendency will make his opinions the rule of judgment, and approve or condemn the sentiments of others only as they shall square with or differ from his own; that it is time enough for the rightful purposes of civil government for its officers to interfere when principles break out into overt acts against peace and good order; and finally, that truth is great and will prevail if left to herself; that she is the proper and sufficient antagonist to error, and has nothing to fear from the conflict unless by human interposition disarmed of her natural weapons, free argument and debate; errors ceasing to be dangerous when it is permitted freely to contradict them.

We the General Assembly of Virginia do enact that no man shall be compelled to frequent or support any religious worship, place, or ministry whatsoever, nor shall be enforced, restrained, molested, or burthened in his body or goods, nor shall otherwise suffer, on account of his religious opinions or belief; but that all men shall be free to profess, and by argument to maintain, their opinions in matters of religion, and that the same shall in no wise diminish, enlarge, or affect their civil capacities.

And though we well know that this Assembly, elected by the people for the ordinary purposes of legislation only, have no power to restrain the acts of succeeding Assemblies, constituted with powers equal to our own, and that therefore to declare this act irrevocable would be of no effect in law; yet we are free to declare, and do declare, that the rights hereby asserted are of the natural rights of mankind, and that if any act shall be hereafter passed to repeal the present or to narrow its operation, such act will be an infringement of natural right.

Questions for Discussion

1. What assumptions does Jefferson make about how human beings think and behave?
2. Why does the bill argue that religious coercion violates God's plan?
3. According to the bill, how does religious establishment end up harming the very churches that it means to support?

Further Reading

Backus, Isaac. "A Door Opened for Equal Christian Liberty." 1783. https://name.umdl.umich.edu/N14086.0001.001.

Barry, John M. *Roger Williams and the Creation of the American Soul: Church, State, and the Birth of Liberty*. Penguin, 2012.

Hall, Mark David, and Daniel L. Dreisbach, eds. *Faith and the Founders of the American Republic*. Oxford University Press, 2014.

Jefferson, Thomas. "Jefferson's Letter to the Danbury Baptists." 1802. https://www.loc.gov/loc/lcib/9806/danpost.html

Kidd, Thomas S. *God of Liberty: A Religious History of the American Revolution*. Basic Books, 2012.

Madison, James. "Memorial and Remonstrance Against Religious Assessments." 1785. https://founders.archives.gov/documents/Madison/01-08-02-0163

Sehat, David. *The Myth of American Religious Freedom*. Oxford University Press, 2011.

Witte, John Witte, Jr., Joel A. Nichols, and Richard W. Garnett, eds. *Religion and the American Constitutional Experiment*, 5th ed. Oxford University Press, 2022.

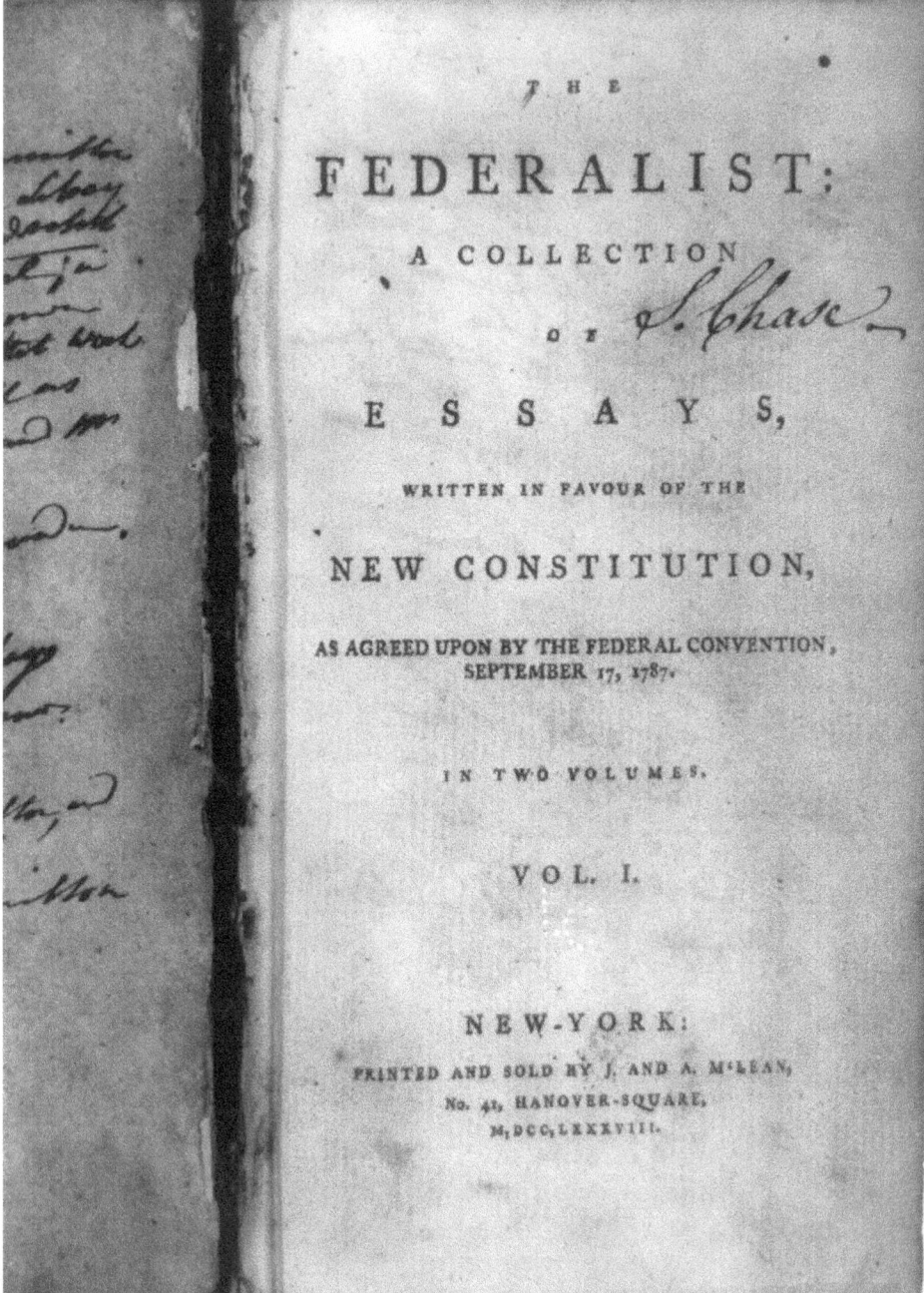

The Federalist Papers were initially published separately. In 1788, the printers J. and A. McLean compiled them into a two-volume collection. It was printed and sold by J. and A. M'Lean at No. 41 Hanover-Square in New York in 1788. (Library of Congress)

4

The Federalist Papers (1787)

James Madison, Alexander Hamilton

Introduction

From May to September of 1787, delegates at the Constitutional Convention in Philadelphia wrestled with the problems that the United States faced under the weak central government prescribed by the Articles of Confederation. The solution they drafted—the Constitution—needed ratification by nine states to become law. Over the next few months, Alexander Hamilton, James Madison, and John Jay got to work persuading Americans that the Constitution was the best plan to govern this sprawling, diverse young nation. (Jay fell ill early in the project and was only able to contribute five essays.)

Under the penname "Publius," they published anonymously in various New York newspapers and later circulated the essays in other parts of the country. The authors used each essay to explain different aspects of the Constitution while also revealing their assumptions about human nature and the lessons of history.

The authors did not agree about everything. They decided it was useful for Americans to encounter multiple points of view. At first, Hamilton, Madison, and Jay read each other's drafts before sending them to the publisher. But time was short, so this practice "was dispensed with. Another reason was that it was found most agreeable to each not to give a positive sanction to all the doctrines and sentiments of the other; there being a known difference in the general complexion of their political theories," Madison later wrote.[1]

The five essays below include some of the authors' most influential ideas. In Federalist #10, Madison discusses methods to keep political factions from running riot and argues that the representative government of a republic is better than direct democracy. In #51, he explains how the Constitution would establish checks and balances between branches of government—a crucial precaution, given his dark view of humanity. "The accumulation of all powers, legislative, executive, and judiciary, in the same hands, whether of one, a few, or many, and whether hereditary, self-appointed, or elective, may justly be pronounced the very definition of tyranny," he writes in another essay.[2]

Hamilton favored a strong executive branch. In #68, he explains the rationale behind choosing the president and vice president by means of an electoral college instead of popular vote, and he goes on in #70 to argue for a powerful president accountable for the government's most important decisions. In #78, he focuses on the judiciary and lays out the principles of judicial review by the courts, which must serve as "bulwarks" against "legislative encroachment on the Constitution."

At a time when skeptics worried that the brand-new country would prove ungovernable, the Federalist Papers made the case for the Constitution as a practical framework built on the values of the American Revolution.— Molly Worthen

James Madison, Federalist Paper #10: The Union as a Safeguard Against Domestic Faction and Insurrection

November 23, 1787

To the People of the State of New York:

AMONG the numerous advantages promised by a well-constructed Union, none deserves to be more accurately developed than its tendency to break and control the violence of faction. The friend of popular governments never finds himself so much alarmed for their character and fate, as when he contemplates their propensity to this dangerous vice. He will not fail, therefore, to set a due value on any plan which, without violating the principles to which he is attached, provides a proper cure for it. The instability, injustice, and confusion introduced into the public councils, have, in truth, been the mortal diseases under which popular governments have everywhere perished; as they continue to be the favorite and fruitful topics from which the adversaries to liberty derive their most specious declamations. The valuable improvements made by the American constitutions on the popular models, both ancient and modern, cannot certainly be too much admired; but it would be an unwarrantable partiality, to contend that they have as effectually obviated the danger on this side, as was wished and expected. Complaints are everywhere heard from our most considerate and virtuous citizens, equally the friends of public and private faith, and of public and personal liberty, that our governments are too unstable, that the public good is disregarded in the conflicts of rival parties, and that measures are too often decided, not according to the rules of justice and the rights of the minor party, but by the superior force of an interested and overbearing majority. However anxiously we may wish that these complaints had no foundation, the evidence, of known facts will not permit us to deny that they are in some degree true. It will be found, indeed, on a candid review of our situation, that some of the distresses under which we labor have been erroneously charged on the operation of our governments; but it will be found, at the same time, that other causes will not alone account for many of our heaviest misfortunes; and, particularly, for that prevailing and increasing distrust of public engagements, and alarm for private rights, which are echoed from one end of the continent to the other. These must be chiefly, if not wholly, effects of the unsteadiness and injustice with which a factious spirit has tainted our public administrations.

By a faction, I understand a number of citizens, whether amounting to a majority or a minority of the whole, who are united and actuated by some common impulse of passion, or of interest, adversed to the rights of other citizens, or to the permanent and aggregate interests of the community.

There are two methods of curing the mischiefs of faction: the one, by removing its causes; the other, by controlling its effects.

There are again two methods of removing the causes of faction: the one, by destroying the liberty which is essential to its existence; the other, by giving to every citizen the same opinions, the same passions, and the same interests.

It could never be more truly said than of the first remedy, that it was worse than the disease. Liberty is to faction what air is to fire, an aliment without which it instantly expires. But it could not be less folly to abolish liberty, which is essential to political life, because it nourishes faction, than it would be to wish the annihilation of air, which is essential to animal life, because it imparts to fire its destructive agency.

The second expedient is as impracticable as the first would be unwise. As long as the reason of man continues fallible, and he is at liberty to exercise it, different opinions will be formed. As long as the connection subsists between his reason and his self-love, his opinions and his passions will have a reciprocal influence on each other; and the former will be objects to which the latter will attach themselves. The diversity in the faculties of men, from which the rights of property originate, is not less an insuperable obstacle to a uniformity of interests. The protection of these faculties is the first object of government. From the protection of different and unequal faculties of acquiring property, the possession of different degrees and kinds of property immediately results; and from the influence of these on the sentiments and views of the respective proprietors, ensues a division of the society into different interests and parties.

The latent causes of faction are thus sown in the nature of man; and we see them everywhere brought into different degrees of activity, according to the different circumstances of civil society. A zeal for different opinions concerning religion, concerning government, and many other points, as well of speculation as of practice; an attachment to different leaders ambitiously contending for pre-eminence and power; or to persons of other descriptions whose fortunes have been interesting to the human passions, have, in turn, divided mankind into parties, inflamed them with mutual animosity, and rendered them much more disposed to vex and oppress each other than to co-operate for their common good. So strong is this propensity of mankind to fall into mutual animosities, that where no substantial occasion presents itself, the most frivolous and fanciful distinctions have been sufficient to kindle their unfriendly passions and excite their most violent conflicts. But the most common and durable source of factions has been the various and unequal distribution of property. Those who hold and those who are without property have ever formed distinct interests in society. Those who are creditors, and those who are debtors, fall under a like discrimination. A landed interest, a manufacturing interest, a mercantile interest, a moneyed interest, with many lesser interests, grow up of necessity in civilized nations, and divide them into different classes, actuated by different sentiments and views. The regulation of these various and interfering interests forms the principal task of modern legislation, and involves the spirit of party and faction in the necessary and ordinary operations of the government.

No man is allowed to be a judge in his own cause, because his interest would certainly bias his judgment, and, not improbably, corrupt his integrity. With equal, nay with greater reason, a body of men are unfit to be both judges and parties at the same time; yet what are many of the most important acts of legislation, but so many judicial determinations, not indeed concerning the rights of single persons, but concerning the rights of large bodies of citizens? And what are the different classes of legislators but advocates and parties to the causes which they determine? Is a law proposed concerning private debts? It is a question to which the creditors are parties on one side and the debtors on the other. Justice ought to hold the balance between them. Yet the parties are, and must be, themselves the judges; and the most numerous party, or, in other words, the most powerful faction must be expected to prevail. Shall domestic manufactures be encouraged, and in what degree, by restrictions on foreign manufactures? are questions which would be differently decided by the landed and the manufacturing classes, and probably by neither with a sole regard to justice and the public good. The apportionment of taxes on the various descriptions of property is an act which seems to require the most exact impartiality; yet there is, perhaps, no legislative act in which greater opportunity and temptation are given to a predominant party to trample on the rules of justice. Every shilling with which they overburden the inferior number, is a shilling saved to their own pockets.

It is in vain to say that enlightened statesmen will be able to adjust these clashing interests, and render them all subservient to the public good. Enlightened statesmen will not always be at the helm. Nor, in many cases, can such an adjustment be made at all without taking into view indirect and remote considerations, which will rarely prevail over the immediate interest which one party may find in disregarding the rights of another or the good of the whole.

The inference to which we are brought is, that the CAUSES of faction cannot be removed, and that relief is only to be sought in the means of controlling its EFFECTS.

If a faction consists of less than a majority, relief is supplied by the republican principle, which enables the majority to defeat its sinister views by regular vote. It may clog the administration, it may convulse the society; but it will be unable to execute and mask its violence under the forms of the Constitution. When a majority is included in a faction, the form of popular government, on the other hand, enables it to sacrifice to its ruling passion or interest both the public good and the rights of other citizens. To secure the public good and private rights against the danger of such a faction, and at the same time to preserve the spirit and the form of popular government, is then the great object to which our inquiries are directed. Let me add that it is the great desideratum by which this form of government can be rescued from the opprobrium under which it has so long labored, and be recommended to the esteem and adoption of mankind.

By what means is this object attainable? Evidently by one of two only. Either the existence of the same passion or interest in a majority at the same time must be prevented, or the majority, having such coexistent passion or interest, must be rendered, by their number and local situation, unable to concert and carry into effect schemes of oppression. If the impulse and the opportunity be suffered to coincide, we well know that neither moral nor religious motives can be relied on as an adequate control. They are not found to be such on the injustice and violence of individuals, and lose their efficacy in proportion to the number combined together, that is, in proportion as their efficacy becomes needful.

From this view of the subject it may be concluded that a pure democracy, by which I mean a society consisting of a small number of citizens, who assemble and administer the government in person, can admit of no cure for the mischiefs of faction. A common passion or interest will, in almost every case, be felt by a majority of the whole; a communication and concert result from the form of government itself; and there is nothing to check the inducements to sacrifice the weaker party or an obnoxious individual. Hence it is that such democracies have ever been spectacles of turbulence and contention; have ever been found incompatible with personal security or the rights of property; and have in general been as short in their lives as they have been violent in their deaths. Theoretic politicians, who have patronized this species of government, have erroneously supposed that by reducing mankind to a perfect equality in their political rights, they would, at the same time, be perfectly equalized and assimilated in their possessions, their opinions, and their passions.

A republic, by which I mean a government in which the scheme of representation takes place, opens a different prospect, and promises the cure for which we are seeking. Let us examine the points in which it varies from pure democracy, and we shall comprehend both the nature of the cure and the efficacy which it must derive from the Union.

The two great points of difference between a democracy and a republic are: first, the delegation of the government, in the latter, to a small number of citizens elected by the rest; secondly, the greater number of citizens, and greater sphere of country, over which the latter may be extended.

The effect of the first difference is, on the one hand, to refine and enlarge the public views, by passing them through the medium of a chosen body of citizens, whose wisdom may best discern the true interest of their country, and whose patriotism and love of justice will be least likely to sacrifice it to temporary or partial considerations. Under such a regulation, it may well happen that the public voice, pronounced by the representatives of the people, will be more consonant to the public good than if pronounced by the people themselves, convened for the purpose. On the other hand, the effect may be inverted. Men of factious tempers, of local prejudices, or of sinister designs, may, by intrigue, by corruption, or by other means, first obtain the suffrages, and then betray the interests, of the people. The question resulting is, whether small or extensive republics are more favorable to the election of proper guardians of the public weal; and it is clearly decided in favor of the latter by two obvious considerations:

In the first place, it is to be remarked that, however small the republic may be, the representatives must be raised to a certain number, in order to guard against the cabals of a few; and that, however large it may be, they must be limited to a certain number, in order to guard against the confusion of a multitude. Hence, the number of representatives in the two cases not being in proportion to that of the two constituents, and being proportionally greater in the small republic, it follows that, if the proportion of fit characters be not less in the large than in the small republic, the former will present a greater option, and consequently a greater probability of a fit choice.

In the next place, as each representative will be chosen by a greater number of citizens in the large than in the small republic, it will be more difficult for unworthy candidates to practice with success the vicious arts by which elections are too often carried; and the suffrages of the people being more free, will be more likely to centre in men who possess the most attractive merit and the most diffusive and established characters.

It must be confessed that in this, as in most other cases, there is a mean, on both sides of which inconveniences will be found to lie. By enlarging too much the number of electors, you render the representatives too little acquainted with all their local circumstances and lesser interests; as by reducing it too much, you render him unduly attached to these, and too little fit to comprehend and pursue great and national objects. The federal Constitution forms a happy combination in this respect; the great and aggregate interests being referred to the national, the local and particular to the State legislatures.

The other point of difference is, the greater number of citizens and extent of territory which may be brought within the compass of republican than of democratic government; and it is this circumstance principally which renders factious combinations less to be dreaded in the former than in the latter. The smaller the society, the fewer probably will be the distinct parties and interests composing it; the fewer the distinct parties and interests, the more frequently will a majority be found of the same party; and the smaller the number of individuals composing a majority, and the smaller the compass within which they are placed, the more easily will they concert and execute their plans of oppression. Extend the sphere, and you take in a greater variety of parties and interests; you make it less probable that a majority of the whole will have a common motive to invade the rights of other citizens; or if such a common motive exists, it will be more difficult for all who feel it to discover their own strength, and to act in unison with each other. Besides other impediments, it may be remarked that, where there is a consciousness of unjust or dishonorable purposes, communication is always checked by distrust in proportion to the number whose concurrence is necessary.

Hence, it clearly appears, that the same advantage which a republic has over a democracy, in controlling the effects of faction, is enjoyed by a large over a small republic;—is enjoyed by the Union over the States composing it. Does the advantage consist in the substitution of representatives whose enlightened views and virtuous sentiments render them superior to local prejudices and schemes of injustice? It will not be denied that the representation of the Union will be most likely to possess these requisite endowments. Does it consist in the greater security afforded by a greater variety of parties, against the event of any one party being able to outnumber and oppress the rest? In an equal degree does the increased variety of parties comprised within the Union, increase this security. Does it, in fine, consist in the greater obstacles opposed to the concert and accomplishment of the secret wishes of an unjust and interested majority? Here, again, the extent of the Union gives it the most palpable advantage.

The influence of factious leaders may kindle a flame within their particular States, but will be unable to spread a general conflagration through the other States. A religious sect may degenerate into a political faction in a part of the Confederacy; but the variety of sects dispersed over the entire face of it must secure the national councils against any danger from that source. A rage for paper money, for an abolition of debts, for an equal division of property, or for any other improper or wicked project, will be less apt to pervade the whole body of the Union than a particular member of it; in the same proportion as such a malady is more likely to taint a particular county or district, than an entire State.

In the extent and proper structure of the Union, therefore, we behold a republican remedy for the diseases most incident to republican government. And according to the degree of pleasure and pride we feel in being republicans, ought to be our zeal in cherishing the spirit and supporting the character of Federalists.

PUBLIUS.

James Madison, Federalist Paper #51: The Structure of the Government Must Furnish the Proper Checks and Balances Between the Different Departments

February 8, 1788

To the People of the State of New York:

TO WHAT expedient, then, shall we finally resort, for maintaining in practice the necessary partition of power among the several departments, as laid down in the Constitution? The only answer that can be given is, that as all these exterior provisions are found to be inadequate, the defect must be supplied, by so contriving the interior structure of the government as that its several constituent parts may, by their mutual relations, be the means of keeping each other in their proper places. Without presuming to undertake a full development of this important idea, I will hazard a few general observations, which may perhaps place it in a clearer light, and enable us to form a more correct judgment of the principles and structure of the government planned by the convention. In order to lay a due foundation for that separate and distinct exercise of the different powers of government, which to a certain extent is admitted on all hands to be essential to the preservation of liberty, it is evident that each department should have a will of its own; and consequently should be so constituted that the members of each should have as little agency as possible in the appointment of the members of the others. Were this principle rigorously adhered to, it would require that all the appointments for the supreme executive, legislative, and judiciary magistracies should be drawn from the same fountain of authority, the people, through channels having no communication whatever with one another. Perhaps such a plan of constructing the several departments would be less difficult in practice than it may in contemplation appear. Some difficulties, however, and some additional expense would attend the execution of it. Some deviations, therefore, from the principle must be admitted. In the constitution of the judiciary department in particular, it might be inexpedient to insist rigorously on the principle: first, because peculiar qualifications being essential in the members, the primary consideration ought to be to select that mode of choice which best secures these qualifications; secondly, because the permanent tenure by which the appointments are held in that department, must soon destroy all sense of dependence on the authority conferring them. It is equally evident, that the members of each department should be as little dependent as possible on those of the others, for the emoluments annexed to their offices. Were the executive magistrate, or the judges, not independent of the legislature in this particular, their independence in every other would be merely nominal. But the great security against a gradual concentration of the several powers in the same department, consists in giving to those who administer each department the necessary constitutional means and personal motives to resist encroachments of the others. The provision for defense must in this, as in all other cases, be made commensurate to the danger of attack. Ambition must be made to counteract ambition. The interest of the man must be connected with the constitutional rights of the place. It may be a reflection on human nature, that such devices should be necessary to control the abuses of government. But what is government itself, but the greatest of all reflections on human nature? If men were angels, no government would be necessary. If angels were to govern men, neither external nor internal controls on government would be necessary. In framing a government which is to be administered by men over men, the great difficulty lies in this: you must first enable the government to control the governed; and in the next place oblige it to control itself. A dependence on the people is, no doubt, the primary control on the government; but experience has taught mankind the necessity of auxiliary precautions. This policy of supplying, by opposite and rival interests, the defect of better motives, might be traced through the whole system of human affairs, private as well as public. We see it particularly displayed in all the subordinate distributions of power, where the constant aim is to divide and arrange the several offices in such a manner as that each may be a check on the other that the private interest of every individual may be a sentinel over the public rights. These inventions of prudence cannot be less requisite in the distribution of the supreme powers of the State. But it is not possible to give to each department an equal power of self-defense. In republican government, the legislative authority necessarily predominates. The remedy for this inconveniency is to divide the legislature into different branches; and to render them, by different modes of election and different principles of action, as little connected with each other as the nature of their common functions and their common dependence on the society will admit. It may even be necessary to guard against dangerous encroachments by still further precautions. As the weight of the legislative authority requires that it should be thus divided, the weakness of the executive may require, on the other hand, that it should be fortified. An absolute negative on the legislature appears, at first view, to be the natural defense with which the executive magistrate should be armed. But perhaps it would be neither altogether safe nor alone sufficient. On ordinary occasions it might not be exerted with the requisite firmness, and on extraordinary occasions it might be perfidiously abused. May not this defect of an absolute negative be supplied by some qualified connection between this weaker department and the weaker branch of the stronger department, by which the latter may be led to support the constitutional rights of the former, without being too much detached from the rights of its own department? If the principles on which these observations are founded be just, as I persuade myself they are, and they be applied as a criterion to the several State constitutions, and to the federal Constitution it will be found that if the latter does not perfectly correspond with them, the former are infinitely less able to bear such a test. There are, moreover, two considerations particularly applicable to the federal system of America, which place that system in a very interesting point of view. First. In a single republic, all the power surrendered by the people is submitted to the administration of a single government; and the usurpations are guarded against by a division of the government into distinct and separate departments. In the compound republic of America, the power surrendered by the people is first divided between two distinct governments, and then the portion allotted to each subdivided among distinct and separate departments. Hence a double security arises to the rights of the people. The different governments will control each other, at the same time that each will be controlled by itself. Second. It is of great importance in a republic not only to guard the society against the oppression of its rulers, but to guard one part of the society against the injustice of the other part. Different interests necessarily exist in different classes of citizens. If a majority be united by a common interest, the rights of the minority will be insecure. There are but two methods of providing against this evil: the one by creating a will in the community independent of the majority that is, of the society itself; the other, by comprehending in the society so many separate descriptions of citizens as will render an unjust combination of a majority of the whole very improbable, if not impracticable. The first method prevails in all governments possessing an hereditary or self-appointed authority. This, at best, is but a precarious security; because a power independent of the society may as well espouse the unjust views of the major, as the rightful interests of the minor party, and may possibly be turned against both parties. The second method will be exemplified in the federal republic of the United States. Whilst all authority in it will be derived from and dependent on the society, the society itself will be broken into so many parts, interests, and classes of citizens, that the rights of individuals, or of the minority, will be in little danger from interested combinations of the majority. In a free government the security for civil rights must be the same as that for religious rights. It consists in the one case in the multiplicity of interests, and in the other in the multiplicity of sects. The degree of security in both cases will depend on the number of interests and sects; and this may be presumed to depend on the extent of country and number of people comprehended under the same government. This view of the subject must particularly recommend a proper federal system to all the sincere and considerate friends of republican government, since it shows that in exact proportion as the territory of the Union may be formed into more circumscribed Confederacies, or States oppressive combinations of a majority will be facilitated: the best security, under the republican forms, for the rights of every class of citizens, will be diminished: and consequently the stability and independence of some member of the government, the only other security, must be proportionately increased. Justice is the end of government. It is the end of civil society. It ever has been and ever will be pursued until it be obtained, or until liberty be lost in the pursuit. In a society under the forms of which the stronger faction can readily unite and oppress the weaker, anarchy may as truly be said to reign as in a state of nature, where the weaker individual is not secured against the violence of the stronger; and as, in the latter state, even the stronger individuals are prompted, by the uncertainty of their condition, to submit to a government which may protect the weak as well as themselves; so, in the former state, will the more powerful factions or parties be gradually induced, by a like motive, to wish for a government which will protect all parties, the weaker as well as the more powerful. It can be little doubted that if the State of Rhode Island was separated from the Confederacy and left to itself, the insecurity of rights under the popular form of government within such narrow limits would be displayed by such reiterated oppressions of factious majorities that some power altogether independent of the people would soon be called for by the voice of the very factions whose misrule had proved the necessity of it. In the extended republic of the United States, and among the great variety of interests, parties, and sects which it embraces, a coalition of a majority of the whole society could seldom take place on any other principles than those of justice and the general good; whilst there being thus less danger to a minor from the will of a major party, there must be less pretext, also, to provide for the security of the former, by introducing into the government a will not dependent on the latter, or, in other words, a will independent of the society itself. It is no less certain than it is important, notwithstanding the contrary opinions which have been entertained, that the larger the society, provided it lie within a practical sphere, the more duly capable it will be of self-government. And happily for the REPUBLICAN CAUSE, the practicable sphere may be carried to a very great extent, by a judicious modification and mixture of the FEDERAL PRINCIPLE.

PUBLIUS.

Alexander Hamilton, Federalist Paper #68: The Mode of Electing the President

March 14, 1788

To the People of the State of New York:

THE mode of appointment of the Chief Magistrate of the United States is almost the only part of the system, of any consequence, which has escaped without severe censure, or which has received the slightest mark of approbation from its opponents. The most plausible of these, who has appeared in print, has even deigned to admit that the election of the President is pretty well guarded.[1] I venture somewhat further, and hesitate not to affirm, that if the manner of it be not perfect, it is at least excellent. It unites in an eminent degree all the advantages, the union of which was to be wished for.

It was desirable that the sense of the people should operate in the choice of the person to whom so important a trust was to be confided. This end will be answered by committing the right of making it, not to any preestablished body, but to men chosen by the people for the special purpose, and at the particular conjuncture.

It was equally desirable, that the immediate election should be made by men most capable of analyzing the qualities adapted to the station, and acting under circumstances favorable to deliberation, and to a judicious combination of all the reasons and inducements which were proper to govern their choice. A small number of persons, selected by their fellow-citizens from the general mass, will be most likely to possess the information and discernment requisite to such complicated investigations.

It was also peculiarly desirable to afford as little opportunity as possible to tumult and disorder. This evil was not least to be dreaded in the election of a magistrate, who was to have so important an agency in the administration of the government as the President of the United States. But the precautions which have been so happily concerted in the system under consideration, promise an effectual security against this mischief. The choice of SEVERAL, to form an intermediate body of electors, will be much less apt to convulse the community with any extraordinary or violent movements, than the choice of ONE who was himself to be the final object of the public wishes. And as the electors, chosen in each State, are to assemble and vote in the State in which they are chosen, this detached and divided situation will expose them much less to heats and ferments, which might be communicated from them to the people, than if they were all to be convened at one time, in one place.

Nothing was more to be desired than that every practicable obstacle should be opposed to cabal, intrigue, and corruption. These most deadly adversaries of republican government might naturally have been expected to make their approaches from more than one quarter, but chiefly from the desire in foreign powers to gain an improper ascendant in our councils. How could they better gratify this, than by raising a creature of their own to the chief magistracy of the Union? But the convention have guarded against all danger of this sort, with the most provident and judicious attention. They have not made the appointment of the President to depend on any preexisting bodies of men, who might be tampered with beforehand to prostitute their votes; but they have referred it in the first instance to an immediate act of the people of America, to be exerted in the choice of persons for the temporary and sole purpose of making the appointment. And they have excluded from eligibility to this trust, all those who from situation might be suspected of too great devotion to the President in office. No senator, representative, or other person holding a place of trust or profit under the United States, can be of the numbers of the electors. Thus without corrupting the body of the people, the immediate agents in the election will at least enter upon the task free from any sinister bias. Their transient existence, and their detached situation, already taken notice of, afford a satisfactory prospect of their continuing so, to the conclusion of it. The business of corruption, when it is to embrace so considerable a number of men, requires time as well as means. Nor would it be found easy suddenly to embark them, dispersed as they would be over thirteen States, in any combinations founded upon motives, which though they could not properly be denominated corrupt, might yet be of a nature to mislead them from their duty.

Another and no less important desideratum was, that the Executive should be independent for his continuance in office on all but the people themselves. He might otherwise be tempted to sacrifice his duty to his complaisance for those whose favor was necessary to the duration of his official consequence. This advantage will also be secured, by making his re-election to depend on a special body of representatives, deputed by the society for the single purpose of making the important choice.

All these advantages will happily combine in the plan devised by the convention; which is, that the people of each State shall choose a number of persons as electors, equal to the number of senators and representatives of such State in the national government, who shall assemble within the State, and vote for some fit person as President. Their votes, thus given, are to be transmitted to the seat of the national government, and the person who may happen to have a majority of the whole number of votes will be the President. But as a majority of the votes might not always happen to centre in one man, and as it might be unsafe to permit less than a majority to be conclusive, it is provided that, in such a contingency, the House of Representatives shall select out of the candidates who shall have the five highest number of votes, the man who in their opinion may be best qualified for the office.

The process of election affords a moral certainty, that the office of President will never fall to the lot of any man who is not in an eminent degree endowed with the requisite qualifications. Talents for low intrigue, and the little arts of popularity, may alone suffice to elevate a man to the first honors in a single State; but it will require other talents, and a different kind of merit, to establish him in the esteem and confidence of the whole Union, or of so considerable a portion of it as would be necessary to make him a successful candidate for the distinguished office of President of the United States. It will not be too strong to say, that there will be a constant probability of seeing the station filled by characters pre-eminent for ability and virtue. And this will be thought no inconsiderable recommendation of the Constitution, by those who are able to estimate the share which the executive in every government must necessarily have in its good or ill administration. Though we cannot acquiesce in the political heresy of the poet who says: "For forms of government let fools contest That which is best administered is best," yet we may safely pronounce, that the true test of a good government is its aptitude and tendency to produce a good administration.

The Vice-President is to be chosen in the same manner with the President; with this difference, that the Senate is to do, in respect to the former, what is to be done by the House of Representatives, in respect to the latter.

The appointment of an extraordinary person, as Vice-President, has been objected to as superfluous, if not mischievous. It has been alleged, that it would have been preferable to have authorized the Senate to elect out of their own body an officer answering that description. But two considerations seem to justify the ideas of the convention in this respect. One is, that to secure at all times the possibility of a definite resolution of the body, it is necessary that the President should have only a casting vote. And to take the senator of any State from his seat as senator, to place him in that of President of the Senate, would be to exchange, in regard to the State from which he came, a constant for a contingent vote. The other consideration is, that as the Vice-President may occasionally become a substitute for the President, in the supreme executive magistracy, all the reasons which recommend the mode of election prescribed for the one, apply with great if not with equal force to the manner of appointing the other. It is remarkable that in this, as in most other instances, the objection which is made would lie against the constitution of this State. We have a Lieutenant-Governor, chosen by the people at large, who presides in the Senate, and is the constitutional substitute for the Governor, in casualties similar to those which would authorize the Vice-President to exercise the authorities and discharge the duties of the President.

PUBLIUS.

[1] Vide FEDERAL FARMER.

Alexander Hamilton, Federalist Paper #70: The Executive Department Further Considered

March 18, 1788

To the People of the State of New York:

THERE is an idea, which is not without its advocates, that a vigorous Executive is inconsistent with the genius of republican government. The enlightened well-wishers to this species of government must at least hope that the supposition is destitute of foundation; since they can never admit its truth, without at the same time admitting the condemnation of their own principles. Energy in the Executive is a leading character in the definition of good government. It is essential to the protection of the community against foreign attacks; it is not less essential to the steady administration of the laws; to the protection of property against those irregular and high-handed combinations which sometimes interrupt the ordinary course of justice; to the security of liberty against the enterprises and assaults of ambition, of faction, and of anarchy. Every man the least conversant in Roman story, knows how often that republic was obliged to take refuge in the absolute power of a single man, under the formidable title of Dictator, as well against the intrigues of ambitious individuals who aspired to the tyranny, and the seditions of whole classes of the community whose conduct threatened the existence of all government, as against the invasions of external enemies who menaced the conquest and destruction of Rome.

There can be no need, however, to multiply arguments or examples on this head. A feeble Executive implies a feeble execution of the government. A feeble execution is but another phrase for a bad execution; and a government ill executed, whatever it may be in theory, must be, in practice, a bad government.

Taking it for granted, therefore, that all men of sense will agree in the necessity of an energetic Executive, it will only remain to inquire, what are the ingredients which constitute this energy? How far can they be combined with those other ingredients which constitute safety in the republican sense? And how far does this combination characterize the plan which has been reported by the convention?

The ingredients which constitute energy in the Executive are, first, unity; secondly, duration; thirdly, an adequate provision for its support; fourthly, competent powers.

The ingredients which constitute safety in the republican sense are, first, a due dependence on the people, secondly, a due responsibility.

Those politicians and statesmen who have been the most celebrated for the soundness of their principles and for the justice of their views, have declared in favor of a single Executive and a numerous legislature. They have with great propriety, considered energy as the most necessary qualification of the former, and have regarded this as most applicable to power in a single hand, while they have, with equal propriety, considered the latter as best adapted to deliberation and wisdom, and best calculated to conciliate the confidence of the people and to secure their privileges and interests.

That unity is conducive to energy will not be disputed. Decision, activity, secrecy, and despatch will generally characterize the proceedings of one man in a much more eminent degree than the proceedings of any greater number; and in proportion as the number is increased, these qualities will be diminished.

This unity may be destroyed in two ways: either by vesting the power in two or more magistrates of equal dignity and authority; or by vesting it ostensibly in one man, subject, in whole or in part, to the control and co-operation of others, in the capacity of counsellors to him. Of the first, the two Consuls of Rome may serve as an example; of the last, we shall find examples in the constitutions of several of the States. New York and New Jersey, if I recollect right, are the only States which have intrusted the executive authority wholly to single men.[1] Both these methods of destroying the unity of the Executive have their partisans; but the votaries of an executive council are the most numerous. They are both liable, if not to equal, to similar objections, and may in most lights be examined in conjunction.

The experience of other nations will afford little instruction on this head. As far, however, as it teaches any thing, it teaches us not to be enamoured of plurality in the Executive. We have seen that the Achaeans, on an experiment of two Praetors, were induced to abolish one. The Roman history records many instances of mischiefs to the republic from the dissensions between the Consuls, and between the military Tribunes, who were at times substituted for the Consuls. But it gives us no specimens of any peculiar advantages derived to the state from the circumstance of the plurality of those magistrates. That the dissensions between them were not more frequent or more fatal, is a matter of astonishment, until we advert to the singular position in which the republic was almost continually placed, and to the prudent policy pointed out by the circumstances of the state, and pursued by the Consuls, of making a division of the government between them. The patricians engaged in a perpetual struggle with the plebeians for the preservation of their ancient authorities and dignities; the Consuls, who were generally chosen out of the former body, were commonly united by the personal interest they had in the defense of the privileges of their order. In addition to this motive of union, after the arms of the republic had considerably expanded the bounds of its empire, it became an established custom with the Consuls to divide the administration between themselves by lot one of them remaining at Rome to govern the city and its environs, the other taking the command in the more distant provinces. This expedient must, no doubt, have had great influence in preventing those collisions and rivalships which might otherwise have embroiled the peace of the republic.

But quitting the dim light of historical research, attaching ourselves purely to the dictates of reason and good sense, we shall discover much greater cause to reject than to approve the idea of plurality in the Executive, under any modification whatever.

Wherever two or more persons are engaged in any common enterprise or pursuit, there is always danger of difference of opinion. If it be a public trust or office, in which they are clothed with equal dignity and authority, there is peculiar danger of personal emulation and even animosity. From either, and especially from all these causes, the most bitter dissensions are apt to spring. Whenever these happen, they lessen the respectability, weaken the authority, and distract the plans and operation of those whom they divide. If they should unfortunately assail the supreme executive magistracy of a country, consisting of a plurality of persons, they might impede or frustrate the most important measures of the government, in the most critical emergencies of the state. And what is still worse, they might split the community into the most violent and irreconcilable factions, adhering differently to the different individuals who composed the magistracy.

Men often oppose a thing, merely because they have had no agency in planning it, or because it may have been planned by those whom they dislike. But if they have been consulted, and have happened to disapprove, opposition then becomes, in their estimation, an indispensable duty of self-love. They seem to think themselves bound in honor, and by all the motives of personal infallibility, to defeat the success of what has been resolved upon contrary to their sentiments. Men of upright, benevolent tempers have too many opportunities of remarking, with horror, to what desperate lengths this disposition is sometimes carried, and how often the great interests of society are sacrificed to the vanity, to the conceit, and to the obstinacy of individuals, who have credit enough to make their passions and their caprices interesting to mankind. Perhaps the question now before the public may, in its consequences, afford melancholy proofs of the effects of this despicable frailty, or rather detestable vice, in the human character.

Upon the principles of a free government, inconveniences from the source just mentioned must necessarily be submitted to in the formation of the legislature; but it is unnecessary, and therefore unwise, to introduce them into the constitution of the Executive. It is here too that they may be most pernicious. In the legislature, promptitude of decision is oftener an evil than a benefit. The differences of opinion, and the jarrings of parties in that department of the government, though they may sometimes obstruct salutary plans, yet often promote deliberation and circumspection, and serve to check excesses in the majority. When a resolution too is once taken, the opposition must be at an end. That resolution is a law, and resistance to it punishable. But no favorable circumstances palliate or atone for the disadvantages of dissension in the executive department. Here, they are pure and unmixed. There is no point at which they cease to operate. They serve to embarrass and weaken the execution of the plan or measure to which they relate, from the first step to the final conclusion of it. They constantly counteract those qualities in the Executive which are the most necessary ingredients in its composition, vigor and expedition, and this without any counterbalancing good. In the conduct of war, in which the energy of the Executive is the bulwark of the national security, every thing would be to be apprehended from its plurality.

It must be confessed that these observations apply with principal weight to the first case supposed that is, to a plurality of magistrates of equal dignity and authority a scheme, the advocates for which are not likely to form a numerous sect; but they apply, though not with equal, yet with considerable weight to the project of a council, whose concurrence is made constitutionally necessary to the operations of the ostensible Executive. An artful cabal in that council would be able to distract and to enervate the whole system of administration. If no such cabal should exist, the mere diversity of views and opinions would alone be sufficient to tincture the exercise of the executive authority with a spirit of habitual feebleness and dilatoriness.

But one of the weightiest objections to a plurality in the Executive, and which lies as much against the last as the first plan, is, that it tends to conceal faults and destroy responsibility.

Responsibility is of two kinds to censure and to punishment. The first is the more important of the two, especially in an elective office. Man, in public trust, will much oftener act in such a manner as to render him unworthy of being any longer trusted, than in such a manner as to make him obnoxious to legal punishment. But the multiplication of the Executive adds to the difficulty of detection in either case. It often becomes impossible, amidst mutual accusations, to determine on whom the blame or the punishment of a pernicious measure, or series of pernicious measures, ought really to fall. It is shifted from one to another with so much dexterity, and under such plausible appearances, that the public opinion is left in suspense about the real author. The circumstances which may have led to any national miscarriage or misfortune are sometimes so complicated that, where there are a number of actors who may have had different degrees and kinds of agency, though we may clearly see upon the whole that there has been mismanagement, yet it may be impracticable to pronounce to whose account the evil which may have been incurred is truly chargeable.

"I was overruled by my council. The council were so divided in their opinions that it was impossible to obtain any better resolution on the point." These and similar pretexts are constantly at hand, whether true or false. And who is there that will either take the trouble or incur the odium, of a strict scrutiny into the secret springs of the transaction? Should there be found a citizen zealous enough to undertake the unpromising task, if there happen to be collusion between the parties concerned, how easy it is to clothe the circumstances with so much ambiguity, as to render it uncertain what was the precise conduct of any of those parties?

In the single instance in which the governor of this State is coupled with a council that is, in the appointment to offices, we have seen the mischiefs of it in the view now under consideration. Scandalous appointments to important offices have been made. Some cases, indeed, have been so flagrant that ALL PARTIES have agreed in the impropriety of the thing. When inquiry has been made, the blame has been laid by the governor on the members of the council, who, on their part, have charged it upon his nomination; while the people remain altogether at a loss to determine, by whose influence their interests have been committed to hands so unqualified and so manifestly improper. In tenderness to individuals, I forbear to descend to particulars.

It is evident from these considerations, that the plurality of the Executive tends to deprive the people of the two greatest securities they can have for the faithful exercise of any delegated power, first, the restraints of public opinion, which lose their efficacy, as well on account of the division of the censure attendant on bad measures among a number, as on account of the uncertainty on whom it ought to fall; and, secondly, the opportunity of discovering with facility and clearness the misconduct of the persons they trust, in order either to their removal from office or to their actual punishment in cases which admit of it.

In England, the king is a perpetual magistrate; and it is a maxim which has obtained for the sake of the public peace, that he is unaccountable for his administration, and his person sacred. Nothing, therefore, can be wiser in that kingdom, than to annex to the king a constitutional council, who may be responsible to the nation for the advice they give. Without this, there would be no responsibility whatever in the executive department an idea inadmissible in a free government. But even there the king is not bound by the resolutions of his council, though they are answerable for the advice they give. He is the absolute master of his own conduct in the exercise of his office, and may observe or disregard the counsel given to him at his sole discretion.

But in a republic, where every magistrate ought to be personally responsible for his behavior in office the reason which in the British Constitution dictates the propriety of a council, not only ceases to apply, but turns against the institution. In the monarchy of Great Britain, it furnishes a substitute for the prohibited responsibility of the chief magistrate, which serves in some degree as a hostage to the national justice for his good behavior. In the American republic, it would serve to destroy, or would greatly diminish, the intended and necessary responsibility of the Chief Magistrate himself.

The idea of a council to the Executive, which has so generally obtained in the State constitutions, has been derived from that maxim of republican jealousy which considers power as safer in the hands of a number of men than of a single man. If the maxim should be admitted to be applicable to the case, I should contend that the advantage on that side would not counterbalance the numerous disadvantages on the opposite side. But I do not think the rule at all applicable to the executive power. I clearly concur in opinion, in this particular, with a writer whom the celebrated Junius pronounces to be "deep, solid, and ingenious," that "the executive power is more easily confined when it is ONE'";[2] that it is far more safe there should be a single object for the jealousy and watchfulness of the people; and, in a word, that all multiplication of the Executive is rather dangerous than friendly to liberty.

A little consideration will satisfy us, that the species of security sought for in the multiplication of the Executive, is unattainable. Numbers must be so great as to render combination difficult, or they are rather a source of danger than of security. The united credit and influence of several individuals must be more formidable to liberty, than the credit and influence of either of them separately. When power, therefore, is placed in the hands of so small a number of men, as to admit of their interests and views being easily combined in a common enterprise, by an artful leader, it becomes more liable to abuse, and more dangerous when abused, than if it be lodged in the hands of one man; who, from the very circumstance of his being alone, will be more narrowly watched and more readily suspected, and who cannot unite so great a mass of influence as when he is associated with others. The Decemvirs of Rome, whose name denotes their number,[3] were more to be dreaded in their usurpation than any ONE of them would have been. No person would think of proposing an Executive much more numerous than that body; from six to a dozen have been suggested for the number of the council. The extreme of these numbers, is not too great for an easy combination; and from such a combination America would have more to fear, than from the ambition of any single individual. A council to a magistrate, who is himself responsible for what he does, are generally nothing better than a clog upon his good intentions, are often the instruments and accomplices of his bad and are almost always a cloak to his faults.

I forbear to dwell upon the subject of expense; though it be evident that if the council should be numerous enough to answer the principal end aimed at by the institution, the salaries of the members, who must be drawn from their homes to reside at the seat of government, would form an item in the catalogue of public expenditures too serious to be incurred for an object of equivocal utility. I will only add that, prior to the appearance of the Constitution, I rarely met with an intelligent man from any of the States, who did not admit, as the result of experience, that the UNITY of the executive of this State was one of the best of the distinguishing features of our constitution.

PUBLIUS.

1 New York has no council except for the single purpose of appointing to offices; New Jersey has a council whom the governor may consult. But I think, from the terms of the constitution, their resolutions do not bind him.
2 De Lolme.
3 Ten.

Alexander Hamilton, Federalist Paper #78: The Judiciary Department
May 28, 1788
To the People of the State of New York:
WE PROCEED now to an examination of the judiciary department of the proposed government.

In unfolding the defects of the existing Confederation, the utility and necessity of a federal judicature have been clearly pointed out. It is the less necessary to recapitulate the considerations there urged, as the propriety of the institution in the abstract is not disputed; the only questions which have been raised being relative to the manner of constituting it, and to its extent. To these points, therefore, our observations shall be confined.

The manner of constituting it seems to embrace these several objects: 1st. The mode of appointing the judges. 2d. The tenure by which they are to hold their places. 3d. The partition of the judiciary authority between different courts, and their relations to each other.

First. As to the mode of appointing the judges; this is the same with that of appointing the officers of the Union in general, and has been so fully discussed in the two last numbers, that nothing can be said here which would not be useless repetition.

Second. As to the tenure by which the judges are to hold their places; this chiefly concerns their duration in office; the provisions for their support; the precautions for their responsibility.

According to the plan of the convention, all judges who may be appointed by the United States are to hold their offices DURING GOOD BEHAVIOR; which is conformable to the most approved of the State constitutions and among the rest, to that of this State. Its propriety having been drawn into question by the adversaries of that plan, is no light symptom of the rage for objection, which disorders their imaginations and judgments. The standard of good behavior for the continuance in office of the judicial magistracy, is certainly one of the most valuable of the modern improvements in the practice of government. In a monarchy it is an excellent barrier to the despotism of the prince; in a republic it is a no less excellent barrier to the encroachments and oppressions of the representative body. And it is the best expedient which can be devised in any government, to secure a steady, upright, and impartial administration of the laws.

Whoever attentively considers the different departments of power must perceive, that, in a government in which they are separated from each other, the judiciary, from the nature of its functions, will always be the least dangerous to the political rights of the Constitution; because it will be least in a capacity to annoy or injure them. The Executive not only dispenses the honors, but holds the sword of the community. The legislature not only commands the purse, but prescribes the rules by which the duties and rights of every citizen are to be regulated. The judiciary, on the contrary, has no influence over either the sword or the purse; no direction either of the strength or of the wealth of the society; and can take no active resolution whatever. It may truly be said to have neither FORCE nor WILL, but merely judgment; and must ultimately depend upon the aid of the executive arm even for the efficacy of its judgments.

This simple view of the matter suggests several important consequences. It proves incontestably, that the judiciary is beyond comparison the weakest of the three departments of power[1]; that it can never attack with success either of the other two; and that all possible care is requisite to enable it to defend itself against their attacks. It equally proves, that though individual oppression may now and then proceed from the courts of justice, the general liberty of the people can never be endangered from that quarter; I mean so long as the judiciary remains truly distinct from both the legislature and the Executive. For I agree, that "there is no liberty, if the power of judging be not separated from the legislative and executive powers."[2] And it proves, in the last place, that as liberty can have nothing to fear from the judiciary alone, but would have every thing to fear from its union with either of the other departments; that as all the effects of such a union must ensue from a dependence of the former on the latter, notwithstanding a nominal and apparent separation; that as, from the natural feebleness of the judiciary, it is in continual jeopardy of being overpowered, awed, or influenced by its co-ordinate branches; and that as nothing can contribute so much to its firmness and independence as permanency in office, this quality may therefore be justly regarded as an indispensable ingredient in its constitution, and, in a great measure, as the citadel of the public justice and the public security.

The complete independence of the courts of justice is peculiarly essential in a limited Constitution. By a limited Constitution, I understand one which contains certain specified exceptions to the legislative authority; such, for instance, as that it shall pass no bills of attainder, no ex-post-facto laws, and the like. Limitations of this kind can be preserved in practice no other way than through the medium of courts of justice, whose duty it must be to declare all acts contrary to the manifest tenor of the Constitution void. Without this, all the reservations of particular rights or privileges would amount to nothing.

Some perplexity respecting the rights of the courts to pronounce legislative acts void, because contrary to the Constitution, has arisen from an imagination that the doctrine would imply a superiority of the judiciary to the legislative power. It is urged that the authority which can declare the acts of another void, must necessarily be superior to the one whose acts may be declared void. As this doctrine is of great importance in all the American constitutions, a brief discussion of the ground on which it rests cannot be unacceptable.

There is no position which depends on clearer principles, than that every act of a delegated authority, contrary to the tenor of the commission under which it is exercised, is void. No legislative act, therefore, contrary to the Constitution, can be valid. To deny this, would be to affirm, that the deputy is greater than his principal; that the servant is above his master; that the representatives of the people are superior to the people themselves; that men acting by virtue of powers, may do not only what their powers do not authorize, but what they forbid.

If it be said that the legislative body are themselves the constitutional judges of their own powers, and that the construction they put upon them is conclusive upon the other departments, it may be answered, that this cannot be the natural presumption, where it is not to be collected from any particular provisions in the Constitution. It is not otherwise to be supposed, that the Constitution could intend to enable the representatives of the people to substitute their WILL to that of their constituents. It is far more rational to suppose, that the courts were designed to be an intermediate body between the people and the legislature, in order, among other things, to keep the latter within the limits assigned to their authority. The interpretation of the laws is the proper and peculiar province of the courts. A constitution is, in fact, and must be regarded by the judges, as a fundamental law. It therefore belongs to them to ascertain its meaning, as well as the meaning of any particular act proceeding from the legislative body. If there should happen to be an irreconcilable variance between the two, that which has the superior obligation and validity ought, of course, to be preferred; or, in other words, the Constitution ought to be preferred to the statute, the intention of the people to the intention of their agents.

Nor does this conclusion by any means suppose a superiority of the judicial to the legislative power. It only supposes that the power of the people is superior to both; and that where the will of the legislature, declared in its statutes, stands in opposition to that of the people, declared in the Constitution, the judges ought to be governed by the latter rather than the former. They ought to regulate their decisions by the fundamental laws, rather than by those which are not fundamental.

This exercise of judicial discretion, in determining between two contradictory laws, is exemplified in a familiar instance. It not uncommonly happens, that there are two statutes existing at one time, clashing in whole or in part with each other, and neither of them containing any repealing clause or expression. In such a case, it is the province of the courts to liquidate and fix their meaning and operation. So far as they can, by any fair construction, be reconciled to each other, reason and law conspire to dictate that this should be done; where this is impracticable, it becomes a matter of necessity to give effect to one, in exclusion of the other. The rule which has obtained in the courts for determining their relative validity is, that the last in order of time shall be preferred to the first. But this is a mere rule of construction, not derived from any positive law, but from the nature and reason of the thing. It is a rule not enjoined upon the courts by legislative provision, but adopted by themselves, as consonant to truth and propriety, for the direction of their conduct as interpreters of the law. They thought it reasonable, that between the interfering acts of an EQUAL authority, that which was the last indication of its will should have the preference.

But in regard to the interfering acts of a superior and subordinate authority, of an original and derivative power, the nature and reason of the thing indicate the converse of that rule as proper to be followed. They teach us that the prior act of a superior ought to be preferred to the subsequent act of an inferior and subordinate authority; and that accordingly, whenever a particular statute contravenes the Constitution, it will be the duty of the judicial tribunals to adhere to the latter and disregard the former.

It can be of no weight to say that the courts, on the pretense of a repugnancy, may substitute their own pleasure to the constitutional intentions of the legislature. This might as well happen in the case of two contradictory statutes; or it might as well happen in every adjudication upon any single statute. The courts must declare the sense of the law; and if they should be disposed to exercise WILL instead of JUDGMENT, the consequence would equally be the substitution of their pleasure to that of the legislative body. The observation, if it prove any thing, would prove that there ought to be no judges distinct from that body.

If, then, the courts of justice are to be considered as the bulwarks of a limited Constitution against legislative encroachments, this consideration will afford a strong argument for the permanent tenure of judicial offices, since nothing will contribute so much as this to that independent spirit in the judges which must be essential to the faithful performance of so arduous a duty.

This independence of the judges is equally requisite to guard the Constitution and the rights of individuals from the effects of those ill humors, which the arts of designing men, or the influence of particular conjunctures, sometimes disseminate among the people themselves, and which, though they speedily give place to better information, and more deliberate reflection, have a tendency, in the meantime, to occasion dangerous innovations in the government, and serious oppressions of the minor party in the community. Though I trust the friends of the proposed Constitution will never concur with its enemies,[3] in questioning that fundamental principle of republican government, which admits the right of the people to alter or abolish the established Constitution, whenever they find it inconsistent with their happiness, yet it is not to be inferred from this principle, that the representatives of the people, whenever a momentary inclination happens to lay hold of a majority of their constituents, incompatible with the provisions in the existing Constitution, would, on that account, be justifiable in a violation of those provisions; or that the courts would be under a greater obligation to connive at infractions in this shape, than when they had proceeded wholly from the cabals of the representative body. Until the people have, by some solemn and authoritative act, annulled or changed the established form, it is binding upon themselves collectively, as well as individually; and no presumption, or even knowledge, of their sentiments, can warrant their representatives in a departure from it, prior to such an act. But it is easy to see, that it would require an uncommon portion of fortitude in the judges to do their duty as faithful guardians of the Constitution, where legislative invasions of it had been instigated by the major voice of the community.

But it is not with a view to infractions of the Constitution only, that the independence of the judges may be an essential safeguard against the effects of occasional ill humors in the society. These sometimes extend no farther than to the injury of the private rights of particular classes of citizens, by unjust and partial laws. Here also the firmness of the judicial magistracy is of vast importance in mitigating the severity and confining the operation of such laws. It not only serves to moderate the immediate mischiefs of those which may have been passed, but it operates as a check upon the legislative body in passing them; who, perceiving that obstacles to the success of iniquitous intention are to be expected from the scruples of the courts, are in a manner compelled, by the very motives of the injustice they meditate, to qualify their attempts. This is a circumstance calculated to have more influence upon the character of our governments, than but few may be aware of. The benefits of the integrity and moderation of the judiciary have already been felt in more States than one; and though they may have displeased those whose sinister expectations they may have disappointed, they must have commanded the esteem and applause of all the virtuous and disinterested. Considerate men, of every description, ought to prize whatever will tend to beget or fortify that temper in the courts: as no man can be sure that he may not be to-morrow the victim of a spirit of injustice, by which he may be a gainer to-day. And every man must now feel, that the inevitable tendency of such a spirit is to sap the foundations of public and private confidence, and to introduce in its stead universal distrust and distress.

That inflexible and uniform adherence to the rights of the Constitution, and of individuals, which we perceive to be indispensable in the courts of justice, can certainly not be expected from judges who hold their offices by a temporary commission. Periodical appointments, however regulated, or by whomsoever made, would, in some way or other, be fatal to their necessary independence. If the power of making them was committed either to the Executive or legislature, there would be danger of an improper complaisance to the branch which possessed it; if to both, there would be an unwillingness to hazard the displeasure of either; if to the people, or to persons chosen by them for the special purpose, there would be too great a disposition to consult popularity, to justify a reliance that nothing would be consulted but the Constitution and the laws.

There is yet a further and a weightier reason for the permanency of the judicial offices, which is deducible from the nature of the qualifications they require. It has been frequently remarked, with great propriety, that a voluminous code of laws is one of the inconveniences necessarily connected with the advantages of a free government. To avoid an arbitrary discretion in the courts, it is indispensable that they should be bound down by strict rules and precedents, which serve to define and point out their duty in every particular case that comes before them; and it will readily be conceived from the variety of controversies which grow out of the folly and wickedness of mankind, that the records of those precedents must unavoidably swell to a very considerable bulk, and must demand long and laborious study to acquire a competent knowledge of them. Hence it is, that there can be but few men in the society who will have sufficient skill in the laws to qualify them for the stations of judges. And making the proper deductions for the ordinary depravity of human nature, the number must be still smaller of those who unite the requisite integrity with the requisite knowledge. These considerations apprise us, that the government can have no great option between fit character; and that a temporary duration in office, which would naturally discourage such characters from quitting a lucrative line of practice to accept a seat on the bench, would have a tendency to throw the administration of justice into hands less able, and less well qualified, to conduct it with utility and dignity. In the present circumstances of this country, and in those in which it is likely to be for a long time to come, the disadvantages on this score would be greater than they may at first sight appear; but it must be confessed, that they are far inferior to those which present themselves under the other aspects of the subject.

Upon the whole, there can be no room to doubt that the convention acted wisely in copying from the models of those constitutions which have established GOOD BEHAVIOR as the tenure of their judicial offices, in point of duration; and that so far from being blamable on this account, their plan would have been inexcusably defective, if it had wanted this important feature of good government. The experience of Great Britain affords an illustrious comment on the excellence of the institution.

PUBLIUS.

[1] The celebrated Montesquieu, speaking of them, says: "Of the three powers above mentioned, the judiciary is next to nothing." "Spirit of Laws." vol. i., page 186.

[2] Idem, page 181.

[3] Vide "Protest of the Minority of the Convention of Pennsylvania," Martin's Speech, etc.

Questions for Discussion

1. What problems do the authors believe the new Constitution will solve?
2. How do Madison and Hamilton understand the goals of the federal government?
3. What assumptions do the authors make about how humans make decisions and handle power?

4. How do their concerns and assumptions compare to those of Americans today?

Further Reading

PRIMARY SOURCES:
The Federalist Papers [complete set, Library of Congress edition].
Samuel Bryan, "Centinel 1" (Anti-Federalist Papers), 1787.
Mercy Otis Warren, *Observations on the New Constitution* (1787).

SECONDARY SOURCES:
Akhil Reed Amar, *The Constitution: A Biography* (Random House, 2005).
H.W. Brands, *Founding Partisans: Hamilton, Madison, Jefferson, Adams and the Brawling Birth of American Politics* (Doubleday, 2023).
Ron Chernow, *Alexander Hamilton* (Penguin, 2005).
Pauline Maier, *Ratification: The People Debate the Constitution, 1787–1788* (Simon & Schuster, 2011).

Notes

1. Fleet, ed., "Madison's Detached Memoranda," *William & Mary Quarterly* (1946), 565.
2. Madison, Federalist 47.

In 1787, Jacob Shallus, a penman, transcribed the text of the constitution on to four sheets of parchment made from treated animal skin using a goose quill and ink made of iron filings in oak gall ink. Shallus's handiwork, for which he received $30, is one of the nation's most valuable documents. (Library of Congress)

5

The Federal Constitution (1789)

The Constitutional Convention

Introduction

The United States Constitution is the foundation of American democracy. The Constitution is the oldest and longest-standing written and codified national constitution in the world. Since its ratification in 1789, it has shaped every facet of American public life and influenced subsequent constitutions across the globe.

The Constitution's Preamble, which is one of the most quoted passages of any American state document, lays out the purposes of the nation's government and the source of its authority:

> We the People of the United States, in Order to form a more perfect Union, establish Justice, insure domestic Tranquility, provide for the common defense, promote the general Welfare, and secure the Blessings of Liberty to ourselves and our Posterity, do ordain and establish this Constitution for the United States of America.

This single sentence encapsulates much of what was innovative about the Constitution when it was adopted. Under the previous national government established by the Articles of Confederation, individual states acted together only for specific purposes. The republic created by the Constitution united citizens as members of a union, with power vested in the new state by the people. The opening words, "We the People," affirm the principle that "the people" and not the states are the source of the national government's legitimacy.

The subsequent articles of the Constitution delineate the organization of the national government while embodying the doctrine of the separation of powers. The government is divided into three branches: the legislative, consisting of the bicameral Congress (Article I); the executive, consisting of the president and subordinate officers (Article II); and the judicial, consisting of the Supreme Court and other federal courts (Article III). The Constitution (in Articles IV, V, and VI) also establishes the framework of American federalism by defining the rights and responsibilities of state governments and the states in relationship to the federal government. The underlying goal is the broad dispersal of power so that there is no locus of concentrated state power.

Since its ratification, the Constitution has been amended twenty-seven times. The first ten amendments, known collectively as the Bill of Rights, place restrictions on the powers of the federal government by offering specific protections of individual liberty and justice. Some of the subsequent amendments clarified or expanded the rights of citizenship, such as the Fourteenth Amendment (which granted equal protection under the law) and the Nineteenth Amendment (which granted the right to vote to women). Other amendments addressed issues that had been ignored or avoided by the original drafters of the Constitution, such as the Thirteenth Amendment (which abolished slavery) and the Sixteenth (which grants Congress the authority to levy personal income taxes). But because the requirements to revise the Constitution are among the most difficult in the world, attempts to amend the Constitution have routinely foundered.

The Constitution has been a flashpoint for public controversy. From its ratification to the present day, some sceptics have complained that the Constitution concentrates too much power in the federal government. Others have criticized it as an impediment to meaningful democracy. Not until more than a century after the ratification of the Constitution did women gain the right to vote. Other undemocratic features, such as the Electoral College and its role in presidential elections as well as the provision of two U.S. senators per state regardless of a state's population, remain in the document to the present.

Yet, the principle of judicial review by federal courts and the Supreme Court provides for the ongoing interpretation of the Constitution and its implications for present-day circumstances. This ongoing interpretation of the Constitution ensures that, even after more than two centuries after its ratification, the document continues to define American democracy.—W. Fitzhugh Brundage

We the People of the United States, in Order to form a more perfect Union, establish Justice, insure domestic Tranquility, provide for the common defense, promote the general Welfare, and secure the Blessings of Liberty to ourselves and our Posterity, do ordain and establish this Constitution for the United States of America.

Article 1

SECTION 1

All legislative Powers herein granted shall be vested in a Congress of the United States, which shall consist of a Senate and House of Representatives.

SECTION 2

The House of Representatives shall be composed of Members chosen every second Year by the People of the several States, and the Electors in each State shall have the Qualifications requisite for Electors of the most numerous Branch of the State Legislature.

No Person shall be a Representative who shall not have attained to the Age of twenty five Years, and been seven Years a Citizen of the United States, and who shall not, when elected, be an Inhabitant of that State in which he shall be chosen.

Representatives and direct Taxes shall be apportioned among the several States which may be included within this Union, according to their respective Numbers, which shall be determined by adding to the whole Number of free Persons, including those bound to Service for a Term of Years, and excluding Indians not taxed, three fifths of all other Persons. The actual Enumeration shall be made within three Years after the first Meeting of the Congress of the United States, and within every subsequent Term of ten Years, in such Manner as they shall by Law direct. The Number of Representatives shall not exceed one for every thirty Thousand, but each State shall have at Least one Representative; and until such enumeration shall be made, the State of New Hampshire shall be entitled to chose three, Massachusetts eight, Rhode Island and Providence Plantations one, Connecticut five, New-York six, New Jersey four, Pennsylvania eight, Delaware one, Maryland six, Virginia ten, North Carolina five, South Carolina five, and Georgia three.

When vacancies happen in the Representation from any State, the Executive Authority thereof shall issue Writs of Election to fill such Vacancies.

The House of Representatives shall chose their Speaker and other Officers; and shall have the sole Power of Impeachment.

SECTION 3

The Senate of the United States shall be composed of two Senators from each State, chosen by the Legislature thereof, for six Years; and each Senator shall have one Vote.

Immediately after they shall be assembled in Consequence of the first Election, they shall be divided as equally as may be into three Classes. The Seats of the Senators of the first Class shall be vacated at the Expiration of the second Year, of the second Class at the Expiration of the fourth Year, and of the third Class at the Expiration of the sixth Year, so that one third may be chosen every second Year; and if Vacancies happen by Resignation, or otherwise, during the Recess of the Legislature of any State, the Executive thereof may make temporary Appointments until the next Meeting of the Legislature, which shall then fill such Vacancies.

No Person shall be a Senator who shall not have attained to the Age of thirty Years, and been nine Years a Citizen of the United States, and who shall not, when elected, be an Inhabitant of that State for which he shall be chosen.

The Vice President of the United States shall be President of the Senate, but shall have no Vote, unless they be equally divided.

The Senate shall chose their other Officers, and also a President pro tempore, in the Absence of the Vice President, or when he shall exercise the Office of President of the United States.

The Senate shall have the sole Power to try all Impeachments. When sitting for that Purpose, they shall be on Oath or Affirmation. When the President of the United States is tried, the Chief Justice shall preside: And no Person shall be convicted without the Concurrence of two thirds of the Members present.

Judgment in Cases of Impeachment shall not extend further than to removal from Office, and disqualification to hold and enjoy any Office of honor, Trust or Profit under the United States: but the Party convicted shall nevertheless be liable and subject to Indictment, Trial, Judgment and Punishment, according to Law.

SECTION 4

The Times, Places and Manner of holding Elections for Senators and Representatives, shall be prescribed in each State by the Legislature thereof;

but the Congress may at any time by Law make or alter such Regulations, except as to the Places of choosing Senators.

The Congress shall assemble at least once in every Year, and such Meeting shall be on the first Monday in December, unless they shall by Law appoint a different Day.

SECTION 5
Each House shall be the Judge of the Elections, Returns and Qualifications of its own Members, and a Majority of each shall constitute a Quorum to do Business; but a smaller Number may adjourn from day to day, and may be authorized to compel the Attendance of absent Members, in such Manner, and under such Penalties as each House may provide.

Each House may determine the Rules of its Proceedings, punish its Members for disorderly Behaviour, and, with the Concurrence of two thirds, expel a Member.

Each House shall keep a Journal of its Proceedings, and from time to time publish the same, excepting such Parts as may in their Judgment require Secrecy; and the Yeas and Nays of the Members of either House on any question shall, at the Desire of one fifth of those Present, be entered on the Journal.

Neither House, during the Session of Congress, shall, without the Consent of the other, adjourn for more than three days, nor to any other Place than that in which the two Houses shall be sitting.

SECTION 6
The Senators and Representatives shall receive a Compensation for their Services, to be ascertained by Law, and paid out of the Treasury of the United States. They shall in all Cases, except Treason, Felony and Breach of the Peace, be privileged from Arrest during their Attendance at the Session of their respective Houses, and in going to and returning from the same; and for any Speech or Debate in either House, they shall not be questioned in any other Place.

No Senator or Representative shall, during the Time for which he was elected, be appointed to any civil Office under the Authority of the United States, which shall have been created, or the Emoluments whereof shall have been encreased during such time; and no Person holding any Office under the United States, shall be a Member of either House during his Continuance in Office.

SECTION 7

All Bills for raising Revenue shall originate in the House of Representatives; but the Senate may propose or concur with Amendments as on other Bills.

Every Bill which shall have passed the House of Representatives and the Senate, shall, before it become a Law, be presented to the President of the United States; If he approve he shall sign it, but if not he shall return it, with his Objections to that House in which it shall have originated, who shall enter the Objections at large on their Journal, and proceed to reconsider it. If after such Reconsideration two thirds of that House shall agree to pass the Bill, it shall be sent, together with the Objections, to the other House, by which it shall likewise be reconsidered, and if approved by two thirds of that House, it shall become a Law. But in all such Cases the Votes of both Houses shall be determined by yeas and Nays, and the Names of the Persons voting for and against the Bill shall be entered on the Journal of each House respectively. If any Bill shall not be returned by the President within ten Days (Sundays excepted) after it shall have been presented to him, the Same shall be a Law, in like Manner as if he had signed it, unless the Congress by their Adjournment prevent its Return, in which Case it shall not be a Law.

Every Order, Resolution, or Vote to which the Concurrence of the Senate and House of Representatives may be necessary (except on a question of Adjournment) shall be presented to the President of the United States; and before the Same shall take Effect, shall be approved by him, or being disapproved by him, shall be repassed by two thirds of the Senate and House of Representatives, according to the Rules and Limitations prescribed in the Case of a Bill.

SECTION 8

The Congress shall have Power To lay and collect Taxes, Duties, Imposts and Excises, to pay the Debts and provide for the common Defense and general Welfare of the United States; but all Duties, Imposts and Excises shall be uniform throughout the United States;

To borrow Money on the credit of the United States;

To regulate Commerce with foreign Nations, and among the several States, and with the Indian Tribes;

To establish a uniform Rule of Naturalization, and uniform Laws on the subject of Bankruptcies throughout the United States;

To coin Money, regulate the Value thereof, and of foreign Coin, and fix the Standard of Weights and Measures;

To provide for the Punishment of counterfeiting the Securities and current Coin of the United States;

To establish Post Offices and post Roads;

To promote the Progress of Science and useful Arts, by securing for limited Times to Authors and Inventors the exclusive Right to their respective Writings and Discoveries;

To constitute Tribunals inferior to the Supreme Court;

To define and punish Piracies and Felonies committed on the high Seas, and Offences against the Law of Nations;

To declare War, grant Letters of Marque and Reprisal, and make Rules concerning Captures on Land and Water;

To raise and support Armies, but no Appropriation of Money to that Use shall be for a longer Term than two Years;

To provide and maintain a Navy;

To make Rules for the Government and Regulation of the land and naval Forces;

To provide for calling forth the Militia to execute the Laws of the Union, suppress Insurrections and repel Invasions;

To provide for organizing, arming, and disciplining, the Militia, and for governing such Part of them as may be employed in the Service of the United States, reserving to the States respectively, the Appointment of the Officers, and the Authority of training the Militia according to the discipline prescribed by Congress;

To exercise exclusive Legislation in all Cases whatsoever, over such District (not exceeding ten Miles square) as may, by Cession of particular States, and the Acceptance of Congress, become the Seat of the Government of the United States, and to exercise like Authority over all Places purchased by the Consent of the Legislature of the State in which the Same shall be, for the Erection of Forts, Magazines, Arsenals, dock-Yards and other needful Buildings;—And

To make all Laws which shall be necessary and proper for carrying into Execution the foregoing Powers, and all other Powers vested by this Constitution in the Government of the United States, or in any Department or Officer thereof.

SECTION 9

The Migration or Importation of such Persons as any of the States now existing shall think proper to admit, shall not be prohibited by the Congress prior to the Year one thousand eight hundred and eight, but a Tax or duty may be imposed on such Importation, not exceeding ten dollars for each Person.

The Privilege of the Writ of Habeas Corpus shall not be suspended, unless when in Cases of Rebellion or Invasion the public Safety may require it.

No Bill of Attainder or ex post facto Law shall be passed.

No Capitation, or other direct, Tax shall be laid, unless in Proportion to the Census or enumeration herein before directed to be taken.

No Tax or Duty shall be laid on Articles exported from any State.

No Preference shall be given by any Regulation of Commerce or Revenue to the Ports of one State over those of another: nor shall Vessels bound to, or from, one State, be obliged to enter, clear, or pay Duties in another.

No Money shall be drawn from the Treasury, but in Consequence of Appropriations made by Law; and a regular Statement and Account of the Receipts and Expenditures of all public Money shall be published from time to time.

No Title of Nobility shall be granted by the United States: And no Person holding any Office of Profit or Trust under them, shall, without the Consent of the Congress, accept of any present, Emolument, Office, or Title, of any kind whatever, from any King, Prince, or foreign State.

SECTION 10

No State shall enter into any Treaty, Alliance, or Confederation; grant Letters of Marque and Reprisal; coin Money; emit Bills of Credit; make any Thing but gold and silver Coin a Tender in Payment of Debts; pass any Bill of Attainder, ex post facto Law, or Law impairing the Obligation of Contracts, or grant any Title of Nobility.

No State shall, without the Consent of the Congress, lay any Imposts or Duties on Imports or Exports, except what may be absolutely necessary for executing it's inspection Laws: and the net Produce of all Duties and Imposts, laid by any State on Imports or Exports, shall be for the Use of the Treasury of the United States; and all such Laws shall be subject to the Revision and Controul of the Congress.

No State shall, without the Consent of Congress, lay any Duty of Tonnage, keep Troops, or Ships of War in time of Peace, enter into any Agreement or Compact with another State, or with a foreign Power, or engage in War, unless actually invaded, or in such imminent Danger as will not admit of delay.

Article II

SECTION I

The executive Power shall be vested in a President of the United States of America. He shall hold his Office during the Term of four Years, and, together with the Vice President, chosen for the same Term, be elected, as follows

Each State shall appoint, in such Manner as the Legislature thereof may direct, a Number of Electors, equal to the whole Number of Senators and Representatives to which the State may be entitled in the Congress: but no Senator or Representative, or Person holding an Office of Trust or Profit under the United States, shall be appointed an Elector.

The Electors shall meet in their respective States, and vote by Ballot for two Persons, of whom one at least shall not be an Inhabitant of the same State with themselves. And they shall make a List of all the Persons voted for, and of the Number of Votes for each; which List they shall sign and certify, and transmit sealed to the Seat of the Government of the United States, directed to the President of the Senate. The President of the Senate shall, in the Presence of the Senate and House of Representatives, open all the Certificates, and the Votes shall then be counted. The Person having the greatest Number of Votes shall be the President, if such Number be a Majority of the whole Number of Electors appointed; and if there be more than one who have such Majority, and have an equal Number of Votes, then the House of Representatives shall immediately choose by Ballot one of them for President; and if no Person have a Majority, then from the five highest on the List the said House shall in like Manner choose the President. But in choosing the President, the Votes shall be taken by States, the Representation from each State having one Vote; A quorum for this Purpose shall consist of a Member or Members from two thirds of the States, and a Majority of all the States shall be necessary to a Choice. In every Case, after the Choice of the President, the Person having the greatest

Number of Votes of the Electors shall be the Vice President. But if there should remain two or more who have equal Votes, the Senate shall choose from them by Ballot the Vice President.

The Congress may determine the Time of choosing the Electors, and the Day on which they shall give their Votes; which Day shall be the same throughout the United States.

No Person except a natural born Citizen, or a Citizen of the United States, at the time of the Adoption of this Constitution, shall be eligible to the Office of President; neither shall any Person be eligible to that Office who shall not have attained to the Age of thirty five Years, and been fourteen Years a Resident within the United States.

In Case of the Removal of the President from Office, or of his Death, Resignation, or Inability to discharge the Powers and Duties of the said Office, the Same shall devolve on the Vice President, and the Congress may by law provide for the Case of Removal, Death, Resignation or Inability, both of the President and Vice President, declaring what Officer shall then act as President, and such Officer shall act accordingly, until the Disability be removed, or a President shall be elected.

The President shall, at stated Times, receive for his Services, a Compensation, which shall neither be increased nor diminished during the Period for which he shall have been elected, and he shall not receive within that Period any other Emolument from the United States, or any of them.

Before he enter on the Execution of his Office, he shall take the following Oath or Affirmation:—I do solemnly swear (or affirm) that I will faithfully execute the Office of President of the United States, and will to the best of my Ability, preserve, protect and defend the Constitution of the United States.

SECTION 2

The President shall be Commander in Chief of the Army and Navy of the United States, and of the Militia of the several States, when called into the actual Service of the United States; he may require the Opinion, in writing, of the principal Officer in each of the executive Departments, upon any Subject relating to the Duties of their respective Offices, and he shall have Power to grant Reprieves and Pardons for Offences against the United States, except in Cases of Impeachment.

He shall have Power, by and with the Advice and Consent of the Senate, to make Treaties, provided two thirds of the Senators present concur; and he shall nominate, and by and with the Advice and Consent of the Senate, shall appoint Ambassadors, other public Ministers and Consuls, Judges of the supreme Court, and all other Officers of the United States, whose Appointments are not herein otherwise provided for, and which shall be established by Law: but the Congress may by Law vest the Appointment of such inferior Officers, as they think proper, in the President alone, in the Courts of Law, or in the Heads of Departments.

The President shall have Power to fill up all Vacancies that may happen during the Recess of the Senate, by granting Commissions which shall expire at the End of their next Session.

SECTION 3

He shall from time to time give to the Congress Information of the State of the Union, and recommend to their Consideration such Measures as he shall judge necessary and expedient; he may, on extraordinary Occasions, convene both Houses, or either of them, and in Case of Disagreement between them, with Respect to the Time of Adjournment, he may adjourn them to such Time as he shall think proper; he shall receive Ambassadors and other public Ministers; he shall take Care that the Laws be faithfully executed, and shall Commission all the Officers of the United States.

SECTION 4

The President, Vice President and all civil Officers of the United States, shall be removed from Office on Impeachment for, and Conviction of, Treason, Bribery, or other high Crimes and Misdemeanors.

Article III

SECTION 1

The judicial Power of the United States, shall be vested in one supreme Court, and in such inferior Courts as the Congress may from time to time ordain and establish. The Judges, both of the supreme and inferior Courts, shall hold their Offices during good Behaviour, and shall, at stated Times, receive for their Services, a Compensation, which shall not be diminished during their Continuance in Office.

SECTION 2

The judicial Power shall extend to all Cases, in Law and Equity, arising under this Constitution, the Laws of the United States, and Treaties made, or which shall be made, under their Authority;—to all Cases affecting Ambassadors, other public Ministers and Consuls; —to all Cases of admiralty and maritime Jurisdiction; —to Controversies to which the United States shall be a Party; —to Controversies between two or more States; —between a State and Citizens of another State; —between Citizens of different States; —between Citizens of the same State claiming Lands under Grants of different States, and between a State, or the Citizens thereof, and foreign States, Citizens or Subjects.

In all Cases affecting Ambassadors, other public Ministers and Consuls, and those in which a State shall be Party, the supreme Court shall have original Jurisdiction. In all the other Cases before mentioned, the supreme Court shall have appellate Jurisdiction, both as to Law and Fact, with such Exceptions, and under such Regulations as the Congress shall make.

The Trial of all Crimes, except in Cases of Impeachment; shall be by Jury; and such Trial shall be held in the State where the said Crimes shall have been committed; but when not committed within any State, the Trial shall be at such Place or Places as the Congress may by Law have directed.

SECTION 3

Treason against the United States, shall consist only in levying War against them, or in adhering to their Enemies, giving them Aid and Comfort. No Person shall be convicted of Treason unless on the Testimony of two Witnesses to the same overt Act, or on Confession in open Court.

The Congress shall have Power to declare the Punishment of Treason, but no Attainder of Treason shall work Corruption of Blood, or Forfeiture except during the Life of the Person attainted.

Article IV

SECTION I

Full Faith and Credit shall be given in each State to the public Acts, Records, and judicial Proceedings of every other State. And the Congress may by general Laws prescribe the Manner in which such Acts, Records and Proceedings shall be proved, and the Effect thereof.

SECTION 2

The Citizens of each State shall be entitled to all Privileges and Immunities of Citizens in the several States.

A Person charged in any State with Treason, Felony, or other Crime, who shall flee from Justice, and be found in another State, shall on Demand of the executive Authority of the State from which he fled, be delivered up, to be removed to the State having Jurisdiction of the Crime.

No Person held to Service or Labor in one State, under the Laws thereof, escaping into another, shall, in Consequence of any Law or Regulation therein, be discharged from such Service or Labor, but shall be delivered up on Claim of the Party to whom such Service or Labour may be due.

SECTION 3

New States may be admitted by the Congress into this Union; but no new State shall be formed or erected within the Jurisdiction of any other State; nor any State be formed by the Junction of two or more States, or Parts of States, without the Consent of the Legislatures of the States concerned as well as of the Congress.

The Congress shall have Power to dispose of and make all needful Rules and Regulations respecting the Territory or other Property belonging to the United States; and nothing in this Constitution shall be so construed as to Prejudice any Claims of the United States, or of any particular State.

SECTION 4

The United States shall guarantee to every State in this Union a Republican Form of Government, and shall protect each of them against Invasion; and on Application of the Legislature, or of the Executive (when the Legislature cannot be convened) against domestic Violence.

Article V

The Congress, whenever two thirds of both Houses shall deem it necessary, shall propose Amendments to this Constitution, or, on the Application of the Legislatures of two thirds of the several States, shall call a Convention for proposing Amendments, which, in either Case, shall be valid to all Intents and Purposes, as Part of this Constitution, when ratified by the Legislatures of three fourths of the several States, or by Conventions in three fourths thereof, as the one or the other Mode of Ratification may be proposed by the Congress; Provided that no Amendment which may be made prior to the Year One thousand eight hundred and eight shall in any Manner affect the first and fourth Clauses in the Ninth Section of the first Article; and that no State, without its Consent, shall be deprived of its equal Suffrage in the Senate.

Article VI

All Debts contracted and Engagements entered into, before the Adoption of this Constitution, shall be as valid against the United States under this Constitution, as under the Confederation.

This Constitution, and the Laws of the United States which shall be made in Pursuance thereof; and all Treaties made, or which shall be made, under the Authority of the United States, shall be the supreme Law of the Land; and the Judges in every State shall be bound thereby, any Thing in the Constitution or Laws of any State to the Contrary notwithstanding.

The Senators and Representatives before mentioned, and the Members of the several State Legislatures, and all executive and judicial Officers, both of the United States and of the several States, shall be bound by Oath or Affirmation, to support this Constitution; but no religious Test shall ever be required as a Qualification to any Office or public Trust under the United States.

Article VII

The Ratification of the Conventions of nine States, shall be sufficient for the Establishment of this Constitution between the States so ratifying the Same.

First Amendment

Congress shall make no law respecting an establishment of religion, or prohibiting the free exercise thereof; or abridging the freedom of speech, or of the press; or the right of the people peaceably to assemble, and to petition the Government for a redress of grievances.

Second Amendment

A well regulated Militia, being necessary to the security of a free State, the right of the people to keep and bear Arms, shall not be infringed.

Third Amendment

No Soldier shall, in time of peace be quartered in any house, without the consent of the Owner, nor in time of war, but in a manner to be prescribed by law.

Fourth Amendment

The right of the people to be secure in their persons, houses, papers, and effects, against unreasonable searches and seizures, shall not be violated, and no Warrants shall issue, but upon probable cause, supported by Oath or affirmation, and particularly describing the place to be searched, and the persons or things to be seized.

Fifth Amendment

No person shall be held to answer for a capital, or otherwise infamous crime, unless on a presentment or indictment of a Grand Jury, except in cases arising in the land or naval forces, or in the Militia, when in actual service in time of War or public danger; nor shall any person be subject for the same offence to be twice put in jeopardy of life or limb; nor shall be compelled in any criminal case to be a witness against himself, nor be deprived of life, liberty, or property, without due process of law; nor shall private property be taken for public use, without just compensation.

Sixth Amendment

In all criminal prosecutions, the accused shall enjoy the right to a speedy and public trial, by an impartial jury of the State and district wherein the crime shall have been committed, which district shall have been previously ascertained by law, and to be informed of the nature and cause of the accusation; to be confronted with the witnesses against him; to have compulsory process for obtaining witnesses in his favor, and to have the Assistance of Counsel for his defence.

Seventh Amendment

In Suits at common law, where the value in controversy shall exceed twenty dollars, the right of trial by jury shall be preserved, and no fact tried by a jury, shall be otherwise re-examined in any Court of the United States, than according to the rules of the common law.

Eighth Amendment

Excessive bail shall not be required, nor excessive fines imposed, nor cruel and unusual punishments inflicted.

Ninth Amendment

The enumeration in the Constitution, of certain rights, shall not be construed to deny or disparage others retained by the people.

Tenth Amendment

The powers not delegated to the United States by the Constitution, nor prohibited by it to the States, are reserved to the States respectively, or to the people.

Eleventh Amendment

The Judicial power of the United States shall not be construed to extend to any suit in law or equity, commenced or prosecuted against one of the United States by Citizens of another State, or by Citizens or Subjects of any Foreign State.

Twelfth Amendment

The Electors shall meet in their respective states and vote by ballot for President and Vice-President, one of whom, at least, shall not be an inhabitant of the same state with themselves; they shall name in their ballots the person voted for as President, and in distinct ballots the person voted for as Vice-President, and they shall make distinct lists of all persons voted for as President, and of all persons voted for as Vice-President, and of the number of votes for each, which lists they shall sign and certify, and transmit sealed to the seat of the government of the United States, directed to the President of the Senate; — the President of the Senate shall, in the presence of the Senate and House of Representatives, open all the certificates and the votes shall then be counted; —The person having the greatest number of votes for President, shall be the President, if such number be a majority of the whole number of Electors appointed; and if no person have such majority, then from the persons having the highest numbers not exceeding three on the list of those voted for as President, the House of Representatives shall choose immediately, by ballot, the President. But in choosing the President, the votes shall be taken by states, the representation from each state having one vote; a quorum for this purpose shall consist of a member or members from two-thirds of the states, and a majority of all the states shall be necessary to a choice. [And if the House of Representatives shall not choose a President whenever the right of choice shall devolve upon them, before the fourth day of March next following, then the Vice-President shall act as President, as in case of the death or other constitutional disability of the President. —] The person having the greatest number of votes as Vice-President, shall be the Vice-President, if such number be a majority of the whole number of Electors appointed, and if no person have a majority, then from the two highest numbers on the list, the Senate shall choose the Vice-President; a quorum for the purpose shall consist of two-thirds of the whole number of Senators, and a majority of the whole number shall be necessary to a choice. But no person constitutionally ineligible to the office of President shall be eligible to that of Vice-President of the United States.

Thirteenth Amendment

SECTION 1
Neither slavery nor involuntary servitude, except as a punishment for crime whereof the party shall have been duly convicted, shall exist within the United States, or any place subject to their jurisdiction.

SECTION 2
Congress shall have power to enforce this article by appropriate legislation.

Fourteenth Amendment

SECTION 1
All persons born or naturalized in the United States, and subject to the jurisdiction thereof, are citizens of the United States and of the State wherein they reside. No State shall make or enforce any law which shall abridge the

privileges or immunities of citizens of the United States; nor shall any State deprive any person of life, liberty, or property, without due process of law; nor deny to any person within its jurisdiction the equal protection of the laws.

SECTION 2

Representatives shall be apportioned among the several States according to their respective numbers, counting the whole number of persons in each State, excluding Indians not taxed. But when the right to vote at any election for the choice of electors for President and Vice-President of the United States, Representatives in Congress, the Executive and Judicial officers of a State, or the members of the Legislature thereof, is denied to any of the male inhabitants of such State, being twenty-one years of age, and citizens of the United States, or in any way abridged, except for participation in rebellion, or other crime, the basis of representation therein shall be reduced in the proportion which the number of such male citizens shall bear to the whole number of male citizens twenty-one years of age in such State.

SECTION 3

No person shall be a Senator or Representative in Congress, or elector of President and Vice-President, or hold any office, civil or military, under the United States, or under any State, who, having previously taken an oath, as a member of Congress, or as an officer of the United States, or as a member of any State legislature, or as an executive or judicial officer of any State, to support the Constitution of the United States, shall have engaged in insurrection or rebellion against the same, or given aid or comfort to the enemies thereof. But Congress may by a vote of two-thirds of each House, remove such disability.

SECTION 4

The validity of the public debt of the United States, authorized by law, including debts incurred for payment of pensions and bounties for services in suppressing insurrection or rebellion, shall not be questioned. But neither the United States nor any State shall assume or pay any debt or obligation incurred in aid of insurrection or rebellion against the United States, or any claim for the loss or emancipation of any slave; but all such debts, obligations and claims shall be held illegal and void.

SECTION 5
The Congress shall have power to enforce, by appropriate legislation, the provisions of this article.

Fifteenth Amendment

SECTION 1
The right of citizens of the United States to vote shall not be denied or abridged by the United States or by any State on account of race, color, or previous condition of servitude–

SECTION 2
The Congress shall have power to enforce this article by appropriate legislation.

Sixteenth Amendment

The Congress shall have power to lay and collect taxes on incomes, from whatever source derived, without apportionment among the several States, and without regard to any census or enumeration.

Seventeenth Amendment

The Senate of the United States shall be composed of two Senators from each State, elected by the people thereof, for six years; and each Senator shall have one vote. The electors in each State shall have the qualifications requisite for electors of the most numerous branch of the State legislatures.

When vacancies happen in the representation of any State in the Senate, the executive authority of such State shall issue writs of election to fill such vacancies: Provided, That the legislature of any State may empower the executive thereof to make temporary appointments until the people fill the vacancies by election as the legislature may direct.

This amendment shall not be so construed as to affect the election or term of any Senator chosen before it becomes valid as part of the Constitution.

Eighteenth Amendment

After one year from the ratification of this article the manufacture, sale, or transportation of intoxicating liquors within, the importation thereof into, or the exportation thereof from the United States and all territory subject to the jurisdiction thereof for beverage purposes is hereby prohibited.

The Congress and the several States shall have concurrent power to enforce this article by appropriate legislation.

This article shall be inoperative unless it shall have been ratified as an amendment to the Constitution by the legislatures of the several States, as provided in the Constitution, within seven years from the date of the submission hereof to the States by the Congress.

Nineteenth Amendment

The right of citizens of the United States to vote shall not be denied or abridged by the United States or by any State on account of sex.

Congress shall have power to enforce this article by appropriate legislation.

Twentieth Amendment

SECTION 1

The terms of the President and the Vice President shall end at noon on the 20th day of January, and the terms of Senators and Representatives at noon on the 3d day of January, of the years in which such terms would have ended if this article had not been ratified; and the terms of their successors shall then begin.

SECTION 2

The Congress shall assemble at least once in every year, and such meeting shall begin at noon on the 3d day of January, unless they shall by law appoint a different day.

SECTION 3

If, at the time fixed for the beginning of the term of the President, the President elect shall have died, the Vice President elect shall become President.

If a President shall not have been chosen before the time fixed for the beginning of his term, or if the President elect shall have failed to qualify, then the Vice President elect shall act as President until a President shall have qualified; and the Congress may by law provide for the case wherein neither a President elect nor a Vice President elect shall have qualified, declaring who shall then act as President, or the manner in which one who is to act shall be selected, and such person shall act accordingly until a President or Vice President shall have qualified.

SECTION 4
The Congress may by law provide for the case of the death of any of the persons from whom the House of Representatives may choose a President whenever the right of choice shall have devolved upon them, and for the case of the death of any of the persons from whom the Senate may choose a Vice President whenever the right of choice shall have devolved upon them.

SECTION 5
Sections 1 and 2 shall take effect on the 15th day of October following the ratification of this article.

SECTION 6
This article shall be inoperative unless it shall have been ratified as an amendment to the Constitution by the legislatures of three-fourths of the several States within seven years from the date of its submission.

Twenty-First Amendment

SECTION 1
The eighteenth article of amendment to the Constitution of the United States is hereby repealed.

SECTION 2
The transportation or importation into any State, Territory, or possession of the United States for delivery or use therein of intoxicating liquors, in violation of the laws thereof, is hereby prohibited.

SECTION 3
This article shall be inoperative unless it shall have been ratified as an amendment to the Constitution by conventions in the several States, as provided in the Constitution, within seven years from the date of the submission hereof to the States by the Congress.

Twenty-Second Amendment

SECTION 1
No person shall be elected to the office of the President more than twice, and no person who has held the office of President, or acted as President, for more than two years of a term to which some other person was elected President shall be elected to the office of the President more than once. But this Article shall not apply to any person holding the office of President when this Article was proposed by the Congress, and shall not prevent any person who may be holding the office of President, or acting as President, during the term within which this Article becomes operative from holding the office of President or acting as President during the remainder of such term.

SECTION 2
This article shall be inoperative unless it shall have been ratified as an amendment to the Constitution by the legislatures of three-fourths of the several States within seven years from the date of its submission to the States by the Congress.

Twenty-Third Amendment

SECTION 1
The District constituting the seat of Government of the United States shall appoint in such manner as Congress may direct:
A number of electors of President and Vice President equal to the whole number of Senators and Representatives in Congress to which the District would be entitled if it were a State, but in no event more than the least populous State; they shall be in addition to those appointed by the States, but they shall be considered, for the purposes of the election of President and Vice President, to be electors appointed by a State; and they shall meet

in the District and perform such duties as provided by the twelfth article of amendment.

SECTION 2
The Congress shall have power to enforce this article by appropriate legislation.

Twenty-Fourth Amendment

SECTION 1
The right of citizens of the United States to vote in any primary or other election for President or Vice President, for electors for President or Vice President, or for Senator or Representative in Congress, shall not be denied or abridged by the United States or any State by reason of failure to pay poll tax or other tax.

SECTION 2
The Congress shall have power to enforce this article by appropriate legislation.

Twenty-Fifth Amendment

SECTION 1
In case of the removal of the President from office or of his death or resignation, the Vice President shall become President.

SECTION 2
Whenever there is a vacancy in the office of the Vice President, the President shall nominate a Vice President who shall take office upon confirmation by a majority vote of both Houses of Congress.

SECTION 3
Whenever the President transmits to the President pro tempore of the Senate and the Speaker of the House of Representatives his written declaration that he is unable to discharge the powers and duties of his office,

and until he transmits to them a written declaration to the contrary, such powers and duties shall be discharged by the Vice President as Acting President.

SECTION 4
Whenever the Vice President and a majority of either the principal officers of the executive departments or of such other body as Congress may by law provide, transmit to the President pro tempore of the Senate and the Speaker of the House of Representatives their written declaration that the President is unable to discharge the powers and duties of his office, the Vice President shall immediately assume the powers and duties of the office as Acting President.

Thereafter, when the President transmits to the President pro tempore of the Senate and the Speaker of the House of Representatives his written declaration that no inability exists, he shall resume the powers and duties of his office unless the Vice President and a majority of either the principal officers of the executive department or of such other body as Congress may by law provide, transmit within four days to the President pro tempore of the Senate and the Speaker of the House of Representatives their written declaration that the President is unable to discharge the powers and duties of his office. Thereupon Congress shall decide the issue, assembling within forty-eight hours for that purpose if not in session. If the Congress, within twenty-one days after receipt of the latter written declaration, or, if Congress is not in session, within twenty-one days after Congress is required to assemble, determines by two-thirds vote of both Houses that the President is unable to discharge the powers and duties of his office, the Vice President shall continue to discharge the same as Acting President; otherwise, the President shall resume the powers and duties of his office.

Twenty-Sixth Amendment

SECTION 1
The right of citizens of the United States, who are eighteen years of age or older, to vote shall not be denied or abridged by the United States or by any State on account of age.

SECTION 2
The Congress shall have power to enforce this article by appropriate legislation.

Twenty-Seventh Amendment

No law, varying the compensation for the services of the Senators and Representatives, shall take effect, until an election of Representatives shall have intervened.

Questions for Discussion

1. Does the Constitution give us our rights and liberties?
2. What powers does the Constitution grant to the national government, and what are the limits on those powers?
3. What powers and duties does the Constitution leave to the individual states?
4. What are examples of the dispersal of power between the branches of the federal government? Why might the drafters of the Constitution make it difficult to amend the Constitution?

Further Reading

The National Archives and Library of Congress provide a wealth of information on the Constitution, its drafting, and its subsequent history at https://www.archives.gov/founding-docs/constitution and https://guides.loc.gov/constitution.

Marbury v. Madison (1803) was a landmark decision of the U.S. Supreme Court that established the principle of judicial review, meaning that federal courts have the power to strike down laws and statutes that violate the Constitution of the United States.

In *Cooper v. Aaron* (1958), the Supreme Court addressed the rights of states in relation to the Tenth Amendment. Following *Brown v. Board of Education* (1954), the school board in Little Rock, Arkansas, filed suit in federal court requesting a delay in implementing desegregation. By the time the case reached the Supreme Court, the case hinged on states' rights and the Tenth Amendment. The Court cited the Supremacy Clause of Article VI, which declares the Constitution to be the supreme law of the land, and *Marbury v. Madison* in holding that the states must abide by the *Brown* decision.

In *Trump v. United States* (2024), the Supreme Court ruled that under the principle of the separation of powers, a former President enjoys absolute immunity from criminal prosecution for all official actions within his constitutional authority.

For a concise survey of the Constitution, consult Ray Raphael, *The U.S. Constitution: Explained—Clause by Clause—for Every American Today* (Vintage, 2017).

PART TWO

A MORE PERFECT UNION

Abraham Lincoln delivers the Gettysburg Address on November 19, 1863.
(printed later, Lincoln's face discovered by Josephine Cobb, 1952)

6

Gettysburg Address (1863)

Abraham Lincoln

Introduction

After two years of fighting, the Civil War had not progressed very well for the Union. Its armies had seized some coastal islands in the Carolinas, captured New Orleans, and penetrated into Northern Mississippi, but in the principal theater, Virginia, Confederate troops had driven back another huge Federal army. In late June 1863, Rebel troops under Gen. R. E. Lee raided through Maryland and into Pennsylvania. Along the Mississippi River, Union forces under Maj. Gen. U. S. Grant struggled to capture Vicksburg and help open the waterway to Union control.

By early July, the course of the war shifted. Grant's army captured Vicksburg and 28,000 Confederates. One day earlier, Federal Maj. Gen. George G. Meade's army repulsed a massive three-day attack at Gettysburg, with combined losses in both armies of over 50,000 men. Although there would be dark days ahead for the Union, it never lost the momentum from the victories at Gettysburg and Vicksburg.

To honor fallen Union soldiers at Gettysburg, various politicians lobbied successfully for the creation of a Soldiers' National Cemetery there. They arranged for a consecration ceremony on November 19, 1863. The schedule that day included prayer and music and highlighted a two-hour oration from Edward Everett, a Northern clergyman, politician, and intellectual. Planners deemed it appropriate that President Abraham Lincoln add a few words. Their guidance was "after the Oration, you, as Chief Executive of the nation, formally set apart these grounds to their sacred use by a few appropriate remarks."[1] Despite a fever and weakness that turned out to be a mild case of smallpox, Lincoln boarded a train for Gettysburg the day before the ceremony. Evidence indicates that he made final additions to his speech on the morning of his presentation.

Both lyrical and majestic, the Gettysburg Address links the Union's cause with the underlying philosophy of the Founding Fathers. Lincoln also demonstrates a breadth of knowledge on the Bible, the antiquities, and other writings in his brief (only 271 words) remarks. Lincoln harkens to the principles expressed in the Declaration of Independence and melded into the very foundation of the U.S. Constitution. He also emphasizes the great experiment called the United States of America. In 1860 Republicans had won the presidency and the House of Representatives in a free and fair election, yet seven Southern states seceded, followed by four more, thereby ripping apart the nation and negating the will of the people under the Constitution. The Union went to war to preserve that government and eliminate the single greatest threat to future unity—slavery.

In the commemoration of the cemetery, Lincoln emphasized the sacrifices that these soldiers made on behalf of those causes. He then called on believers in the Union to redouble their efforts not just to honor the dead but also to restore the nation that had and would continue to serve as a beacon of light to future generations, ensuring that this republic can overcome the calamity of rebellion and preserve the principles that those Founders espoused and fought to achieve.

The initial reaction to Lincoln's Gettysburg Address was mixed along party lines. Yet the next day Everett wrote Lincoln, stating, "I should be glad if I could flatter myself that I came as near to the central idea of the occasion, in two hours, as you did in two minutes."[2] In time the speech emerged as the most concise and powerful statement of what the United States represented.—Joseph T. Glatthaar

Four score and seven years ago our fathers brought forth on this continent, a new nation, conceived in liberty, and dedicated to the proposition that all men are created equal. Now we are engaged in a great civil war, testing whether that nation, or any nation so conceived and so dedicated, can long endure. We are met on a great battlefield of that war. We have come to dedicate a portion of that field as a final resting place for those who here gave their lives that that nation might live. It is altogether fitting and proper that we should do this. But in a larger sense we cannot dedicate, we cannot consecrate, we cannot hallow this ground. The brave men, living and dead, who struggled here have consecrated it, far above our poor power to add or detract. The world will little note, nor long remember, what we say here, but it can never forget what they did here. It is for us the living, rather, to be dedicated here to the unfinished work which they who fought here have thus far so nobly advanced. It is rather for us to be here dedicated to the great task remaining before us, that from these honored dead we take increased devotion to that cause for which they gave the last full measure of devotion, that we here highly resolve that these dead shall not have died in vain, that this nation, under God, shall have a new birth of freedom, and that government of the people, by the people, for the people, shall not perish from the earth.[3]

Questions for Discussion

1. Why did Lincoln link the Union's cause with the documents of the Founding Fathers?
2. Why did Lincoln suggest that the United States was a great experiment in liberty and republicanism?
3. In what ways did Lincoln articulate his vision of the United States in the Gettysburg Address?
4. What did the Union represent in the minds and hearts of Lincoln and the northern people?
5. Why is it important to honor those who gave their lives for the United States?

Further Reading

Conant, Sean, ed. *The Gettysburg Address: Perspectives on Lincoln's Greatest Speech.* Oxford University Press, 2015.

McPherson, James B. *Hallowed Ground: A Walk at Gettysburg.* Crown Publishers, 2003.

Simon, John Y., Harold Holtzer, and William D. Pederson. *The Lincoln Forum: Abraham Lincoln, Gettysburg, and the Civil War.* Savas Publishing, 1999.

Wills, Garry. *Lincoln at Gettysburg: The Words That Remade America.* Simon & Schuster, 1992.

Notes

1. David Wills to Abraham Lincoln, November 2, 1863. https://www.loc.gov/resource/mal.2778100/

2. Edward Everett to Abraham Lincoln, November 20, 1863. https://www.loc.gov/resource/mal.2813300/

3. Five different versions of the address have survived. The one printed here is the most widely accepted version of Lincoln's presentation. See http://www.loc.gov/resource/rbpe.24404500.

In this photograph of President Abraham Lincoln delivering his second inaugural address, Lincoln stands in the center, with papers in his hand. Among those listening to Lincoln and captured in the photograph was actor John Wilkes Booth, who, just over a month later, assassinated the president. (Gardner, Alexander, 1821-1882, Library of Congress.)

7

Abraham Lincoln's Second Inaugural Address (1865)

Abraham Lincoln

Introduction

Although only 701 words long, Lincoln's Second Inaugural Address contains some of the most memorable phrases in American political oratory. On March 4, 1865, before a crowd of about 40,000 spectators who gathered on the steps of the Capitol, Lincoln took seven minutes to deliver his address. Four years earlier he had taken thirty-five minutes to deliver his First Inaugural Address.

The month before, a Union army led by General William Tecumseh Sherman began slashing its way through South Carolina after having cut a swath across Georgia. Meanwhile, Union General Ulysses S. Grant had trapped Confederate General Robert E. Lee's army twenty miles south of Richmond. The Confederacy was on the precipice of complete defeat.

Lincoln might have been expected to deliver a triumphant speech. Instead, the dominant mood of his address was sorrowful. He refrained from gloating about his reelection in the face of daunting odds. Nor did he boast about the Union's pending victory over the southern rebellion. Instead, he used the occasion to share his most profound reflections on the causes and meaning of the war.

Lincoln crafted his speech with evident care, with an eye toward the import of his words and the various audiences he hoped to reach. His language is sparse and concise. The speech consists of twenty-five sentences arranged in four paragraphs. Three quarters of the words in the address are of one syllable. Even more striking, Lincoln mentions God fourteen times, quotes scripture four times, and invokes prayer three times. By doing so, Lincoln broke with the precedent established by his eighteen forerunners in the White House, only one of whom had quoted (in passing) the Bible.

Lincoln calls for reflection, compassion, and humility. He wonders why God allowed the war to come and why it assumed the tragic dimensions it had taken. The "scourge of war," he contends, was divine punishment for the sin of slavery, a sin in which all Americans, North as well as South, were complicit. "Slaves," he explains, "constituted a peculiar and powerful interest. All knew that this interest was somehow the cause of the war." The nation bore a moral debt created by the "bondsmen's 250 years of unrequited toil." While discussing this debt, Lincoln laments those who had wrung "their bread from the sweat of other men's faces," an allusion to the Fall of Man in the Book of Genesis (Genesis 3:19).

Turning from the republic's original sin of slavery, Lincoln ends with a call for compassion and reconciliation. He pleads, "but let us judge not, that we be not judged," an allusion to the words of Jesus in Matthew 7:1. And in one of the most famous passages in the address, Lincoln reworks Psalm 147:3 while urging his fellow Americans to "bind up the nation's wounds."

We can only speculate as to how Lincoln might have applied the principles he invoked in his Second Inaugural Address to the challenges of reuniting a war-scarred nation. Some commentators have interpreted his speech as a promise of a lenient policy toward the defeated rebels. Yet, even while Lincoln emphasized that God's purposes are not directly knowable to humans, he acknowledged with greater clarity and purpose than any previous or subsequent president the unmistakable evil of slavery and its warping of American institutions and values.—W. Fitzhugh Brundage

Fellow countrymen:

At this second appearing to take the oath of the presidential office, there is less occasion for an extended address than there was at the first. Then a statement, somewhat in detail, of a course to be pursued, seemed fitting and proper. Now, at the expiration of four years, during which public declarations have been constantly called forth on every point and phase of the great contest which still absorbs the attention, and engrosses the energies of the nation, little that is new could be presented. The progress of our arms, upon which all else chiefly depends, is as well known to the public as to myself; and it is, I trust, reasonably satisfactory and encouraging to all. With high hope for the future, no prediction in regard to it is ventured.

On the occasion corresponding to this four years ago, all thoughts were anxiously directed to an impending civil-war. All dreaded it—all sought to avert it. While the inaugural address was being delivered from this place, devoted altogether to saving the Union without war, insurgent agents were in the city seeking to destroy it without war—seeking to dissolve the Union, and divide effects by negotiation. Both parties deprecated war; but one of them would make war rather than let the nation survive; and the other would accept war rather than let it perish. And the war came.

One eighth of the whole population were colored slaves, not distributed generally over the union, but localized in the Southern half part of it. These slaves constituted a peculiar and powerful interest. All knew that this interest was, somehow, the cause of the war. To strengthen, perpetuate, and extend this interest was the object for which the insurgents would rend the Union even by war ;while the government claimed no right to do more than to restrict the territorial enlargement of it. Neither party expected for the war, the magnitude, or the duration, which it has already attained. Neither anticipated that the cause of the conflict might cease with or even before the conflict itself should cease. Each looked for an easier triumph, and a result less fundamental and astounding. Both read the same Bible, and pray to the same God; and each invokes His aid against the other. It may seem strange that any men should dare to ask a just God's assistance in wringing their bread from the sweat of other men's faces; but let us judge not that we be not judged. The prayers of both could not be answered; that of neither has been answered fully. The Almighty has His own purposes. "Woe unto the world because of offences for it must needs be that offences come; but woe to that man by whom the offence cometh." If we shall suppose that American Slavery is one of those offences which, in the providence of God, must needs come, but which, having continued through His appointed time, He now wills to remove, and that He gives to both North and South, this terrible war as the woe due to those by whom the offence came, shall we discern therein any departure from those divine attributes which the believers in a living God always ascribe to Him? Fondly do we hope—fervently do we pray—that this mighty scourge of war may speedily pass away. Yet, if God wills that it continue, until all the wealth piled by the bond-man's two hundred and fifty years of unrequited toil shall be sunk, and until every drop of blood drawn with the lash, shall be paid by another drawn with the sword, as was said three thousand years ago, so still it must be said "the judgments of the Lord, are true and righteous altogether."

With malice toward none; with charity for all; with firmness in the right, as God gives us to see the right, let us strive on to finish the work we are in; to bind up the nation's wounds; to care for him who shall have borne the battle, and for his widow, and his orphan—to do all which may achieve and cherish a just and lasting peace, among ourselves, and with the world, all nations.

Questions for Discussion

1. To whom was Lincoln directing his Second Inaugural Address?
2. Why might Lincoln have elected to deliver such a short Second Inaugural Address?
3. Why is the four-word sentence "And the war came" one of the most important statements in Lincoln's Second Inaugural Address?
4. When and why did Lincoln use the words "all" and "both" in his Second Inaugural Address?
5. Why did Lincoln refer to "American slavery" when he introduced the topic of slavery in his address?
6. Lincoln had the reputation for being an unchurched "free-thinker." Nevertheless, his Second Inaugural Address is built on a foundation of Biblical references. Why might Lincoln have invoked familiar Bible passages in his speech?
7. In his Gettysburg Address, Lincoln did not mention slavery. In his Second Inaugural Address, delivered fifteen months later, Lincoln emphasized the centrality of slavery in the nation's history. What may explain this difference in the two speeches?

Further Reading

Burt, John. "Collective Guilt in Lincoln's Second Inaugural Address." *American Political Thought* 4 (Summer 2015): 467–488.
Gardner, Alexander. "Abraham Lincoln Delivering his Second Inaugural Address." 1865. Photograph. http://loc.gov/pictures/resource/ppmsca.23718/
Lincoln, Abraham. Second Inaugural Address. 1865. Reading copy. https://www.loc.gov/resource/mal.4361300/
Morel, Lucas. "Of Justice and Mercy in Abraham Lincoln's Second Inaugural Address." *American Political Thought* 4 (Summer 2015): 455–466.
White, Ronald C., Jr., *Lincoln's Greatest Speech: The Second Inaugural*. Simon & Schuster, 2002.

LADIES' DEPARTMENT.

[BY REQUEST.]

LECTURE
Delivered at the Franklin Hall, Boston, September 21st, 1832.

BY MRS. MARIA W. STEWART.

Why sit we here and die? If we say we will go to a foreign land, the famine and the pestilence are there, and there we shall die. If we sit here, we shall die. Come, let us plead our cause before the whites: if they save us alive, we shall live—and if they kill us, we shall but die.

Maria W. Stewart, "Lecture Delivered at the Franklin Hall, Boston, September 21st, 1832," (The Liberator, November 17, 1832.)

8

Lecture Delivered at Franklin Hall (1832)
Maria W. Stewart

Introduction

Maria W. Stewart, a prominent abolitionist writer and speaker, was the first African American woman to author and publish her own political tract and one of the first women in the United States to give a public address. Born in Connecticut in 1803 to free Black parents, Stewart was orphaned by the age of five and "bound out" as an indentured servant to a minister until she was about fifteen. Stewart left Hartford for Boston, where she found work as a domestic servant, furthering her education along the way through Sunday School classes on religion and reading.

Stewart and her husband, the shipping agent and War of 1812 veteran James W. Stewart, whom she wed in 1826, were part of Boston's free Black community: a small but spirited group that fought segregation and racism. The deaths of her husband in 1829, and less than a year later, of her mentor, the Black abolitionist David Walker, drew Stewart deeper into abolitionist activism and writing. In 1831 Stewart published a widely read essay in *The Liberator* titled "Religion and the Pure Principles of Morality, the Sure Foundation on Which We Must Build." Over the next two years, she delivered four recorded public lectures including this one.

Stewart is the first known woman in the United States to make public addresses to mixed audiences of Black and white men and women, and she faced intense criticism for it. The very act of public speaking was thought to demonstrate a woman's immorality, thereby invalidating anything she had to say. "I have made myself contemptible in the eyes of many," she wrote. "This is the land of freedom," she added, "and we claim our rights," including the right to speak out. Asserting that Black women could lead the fight against exploitation—a role she believed God intended for them—Stewart thus enacted the equality her speeches and essays demanded. She deployed Biblical imagery to encourage Black audiences to seek education and political rights and prodded whites to understand that Black people loved freedom with equal fervor. Stewart's influential style of oratory and argument drew many into the abolitionist movement. After public pressure convinced Stewart to retire from lecturing in 1833, she focused on publishing and teaching.

In this speech delivered to the New England Anti-Slavery Society, Stewart called not only for the abolition of slavery but for Black women to have equal education and opportunities so that they could be equal citizens in the United States. This address reached wider audiences when it was printed in *The Liberator* and when Stewart included it in a collection she published of her writings and speeches.—Katherine Turk

Why sit ye here and die? If we say we will go to a foreign land, the famine and the pestilence are there, and there we shall die. If we sit here, we shall die. Come let us plead our cause before the whites: if they save us alive, we shall live—and if they kill us, we shall but die.

Methinks I heard a spiritual interrogation—"Who shall go forward, and take off the reproach that is cast upon the people of color? Shall it be a woman?" And my heart made this reply—"If it is thy will, be it even so, Lord Jesus!"

I have heard much respecting the horrors of slavery; but may Heaven forbid that the generality of my color throughout these United States should experience any more of its horrors than to be a servant of servants, or hewers of wood and drawers of water! Tell us no more of southern slavery; for with few exceptions, . . . I consider our condition but little better than that. Yet, after all, methinks there are no chains so galling as the chains of ignorance—no fetters so binding as those that bind the soul, and exclude it from the vast field of useful and scientific knowledge. O, had I received the advantages of early education, my ideas would, ere now, have expanded far and wide; but, alas! I possess nothing but moral capability—no teachings but the teachings of the Holy Spirit.

I have asked several individuals of my sex, who transact business for themselves, if providing our girls were to give them the most satisfactory references, they would not be willing to grant them an equal opportunity with others? Their reply has been—for their own part, they had no objection; but as it was not the custom, were they to take them into their employ, they would be in danger of losing the public patronage.

And such is the powerful force of prejudice. Let our girls possess what amiable qualities of soul they may; let their characters be fair and spotless as innocence itself; let their natural taste and ingenuity be what they may; it is impossible for scarce an individual of them to rise above the condition of servants. Ah! why is this cruel and unfeeling distinction? Is it merely because God has made our complexion to vary? If it be, O shame to soft, relenting humanity! . . .

Few white persons of either sex, who are calculated for any thing else, are willing to spend their lives and bury their talents in performing mean, servile labor. And such is the horrible idea that I entertain respecting a life of servitude, that if I conceived of there being no possibility of my rising above the condition of a servant, I would gladly hail death as a welcome messenger. O, horrible idea, indeed! to possess noble souls aspiring after high and honorable acquirements, yet confined by the chains of ignorance and poverty to lives of continual drudgery and toil. Neither do I know of any who have enriched themselves by spending their lives as house-domestics, washing windows, shaking carpets, brushing boots, or tending upon gentlemen's tables. I can but die for expressing my sentiments; and I am as willing to die by the sword as the pestilence; for I am a true born American; your blood flows in my veins, and your spirit fires my breast.

. . . Take us generally as a people, we are neither lazy nor idle; and considering how little we have to excite or stimulate us, I am almost astonished that there are so many industrious and ambitious ones to be found; although I acknowledge, with extreme sorrow, that there are some who never were and never will be serviceable to society. And have you not a similar class among yourselves?

. . . the whites have so long and so loudly proclaimed the theme of equal rights and privileges, that our souls have caught the flame also, ragged as we are. As far as our merit deserves, we feel a common desire to rise above the condition of servants and drudges. I have learnt, by bitter experience, that continual hard labor deadens the energies of the soul, and benumbs the faculties of the mind; the ideas become confined, the mind barren, and, like the scorching sands of Arabia, produces nothing; or, like the uncultivated soil, brings forth thorns and thistles.

Again, continual hard labor irritates our tempers and sours our dispositions; the whole system becomes worn out with toil and fatigue; nature herself becomes almost exhausted, and we care but little whether we live or die. It is true, that the free people of color throughout these United States are neither bought nor sold, nor under the lash of the cruel driver;

many obtain a comfortable support; but few, if any, have an opportunity of becoming rich and independent; and the employments we most pursue are as unprofitable to us as the spider's web or the floating bubbles that vanish into air. As servants, we are respected; but let us presume to aspire any higher, our employer regards us no longer. And were it not that the King eternal has declared that Ethiopia shall stretch forth her hands unto God, I should indeed despair.

I do not consider it derogatory, my friends, for persons to live out to service. There are many whose inclination leads them to aspire no higher; and I would highly commend the performance of almost any thing for an honest livelihood; but where constitutional strength is wanting, labor of this kind, in its mildest form, is painful. And doubtless many are the prayers that have ascended to Heaven from Afric's daughters for strength to perform their work. Oh, many are the tears that have been shed for the want of that strength! Most of our color have dragged out a miserable existence of servitude from the cradle to the grave. And what literary acquirements can be made, or useful knowledge derived, from either maps, books or charts, by those who continually drudge from Monday morning until Sunday noon? O, ye fairer sisters, whose hands are never soiled, whose nerves and muscles are never strained, go learn by experience! Had we had the opportunity that you have had, to improve our moral and mental faculties, what would have hindered our intellects from being as bright, and our manners from being as dignified as yours? Had it been our lot to have been nursed in the lap of affluence and ease, and to have basked beneath the smiles and sunshine of fortune, should we not have naturally supposed that we were never made to toil? And why are not our forms as delicate, and our constitutions as slender, as yours? Is not the workmanship as curious and complete? Have pity upon us, have pity upon us, O ye who have hearts to feel for other's woes; for the hand of God has touched us. Owing to the disadvantages under which we labor, there are many flowers among us that are

... born to bloom unseen,

And waste their fragrance on the desert air.

My beloved brethren, as Christ has died in vain for those who will not accept of offered mercy, so will it be vain for the advocates of freedom to spend their breath in our behalf, unless with united hearts and souls you make some mighty efforts to raise your sons and daughters from the horrible state of servitude and degradation in which they are placed. It is upon you that woman depends; she can do but little besides using her influence; and it is for her sake and yours that I have come forward and made myself a hissing and a reproach among the people; for I am also one of the wretched and miserable daughters of the descendants of fallen Africa. Do you ask, why are you wretched and miserable? I reply, look at many of the most worthy and interesting of us doomed to spend our lives in gentlemen's kitchens. Look at our young men, smart, active and energetic, with souls filled with ambitious fire; if they look forward, alas! what are their prospects? They can be nothing but the humblest laborers, on account of their dark complexions; hence many of them lose their ambition, and become worthless. Look at our middle-aged men, clad in their rusty plaids and coats; in winter, every cent they earn goes to buy their wood and pay their rents; their poor wives also toil beyond their strength, to help support their families. Look at our aged sires, whose heads are whitened with the frosts of seventy winters, with their old wood-saws on their backs. Alas, what keeps us so? Prejudice, ignorance and poverty. But ah! methinks our oppression is soon to come to an end; yea, before the Majesty of heaven, our groans and cries have reached the ears of the Lord of Sabaoth. As the prayers and tears of Christians will avail the finally impenitent nothing; neither will the prayers and tears of the friends of humanity avail us any thing, unless we possess a spirit of virtuous emulation within our breasts. Did the pilgrims, when they first landed on these shores, quietly compose themselves, and say, "the Britons have all the money and all the power, and we must continue their servants forever?" Did they sluggishly sigh and say, "our lot is hard, the Indians own the soil, and we cannot cultivate it?" No; they first made powerful efforts to raise themselves, and then God raised up those illustrious patriots, WASHINGTON and LAFAYETTE, to assist and defend them. And, my brethren, have you made a powerful effort? Have you prayed the Legislature for mercy's sake to grant you all the rights and privileges of free citizens, that your daughters may rise to that degree of respectability which true merit deserves, and your sons above the servile situations which most of them fill?

Questions for Discussion

1. How does Stewart justify her authority to speak?
2. What similarities does Stewart observe between the lives of enslaved and free Black people?

3. Stewart's address is to a society dedicated to the abolition of enslavement, but how does she support her claim that that goal is not sufficient?
4. In Stewart's account, how has racism hampered the progress of Black women and men, and how would Americans' closer adherence to their own founding political values boost the prospects of Black people and strengthen the nation overall?
5. What role does education play in Stewart's ideal society?
6. How does Stewart characterize the relationship between religious authority and political authority, and how does she urge her audience to engage with each?

Further Reading

Harper, Frances Ellen Watkins. "We Are All Bound Up Together." 1866.
New York State Married Women's Property Act of 1848.
Stanton, Elizabeth Cady. "The Seneca Falls Declaration." 1848.
Truth, Sojourner. "Address to the First Annual Meeting of the American Equal Rights Association." 1867.
Walker, David. *Walker's Appeal, in Four Articles; Together with a Preamble, to the Coloured Citizens of the World, but in Particular, and Very Expressly, to Those of the United States of America.* 1829.

Note

1. Stewart's paraphrase of Thomas Gray's poem "Elegy Written in a Country Churchyard," 1751, which reads "Full many a flow'r is born to blush unseen,/And waste its sweetness on the desert air."

A portrait of Frederick Douglass created in 1845. (Library of Congress)

9
What to the Slave is the Fourth of July? (1852)
Frederick Douglass

Introduction

Frederick Douglass was born enslaved in Maryland around 1818 but liberated himself and escaped to the North when he was about twenty years old. Living in free states and encouraged to tell his story, he became an abolitionist and prolific advocate for civil rights for Black people, women, and even Chinese immigrants.[1] In 1852, the Rochester Ladies' Anti-Slavery Society invited him to speak for Independence Day. An excerpt of his speech is available below. When Douglass took the podium, he told his audience that he could not remember "ever to have appeared as a speaker before any assembly more shrinkingly, nor with greater distrust of my ability" than he did at that moment. He offered some reflections on American independence and the generation that won it before delivering a strident critique of the celebrations around the holiday. In the full speech, he also criticizes the Fugitive Slave Law and American Christianity's hypocrisy about slavery. Ever the talented writer, Douglass did not miss the opportunity to provide his audience with some hopeful notes.—Antwain K. Hunter

. . . I am glad, fellow-citizens, that your nation is so young. Seventy-six years, though a good old age for a man, is but a mere speck in the life of a nation. Three score years and ten is the allotted time for individual men; but nations number their years by thousands. According to this fact, you are, even now, only in the beginning of your national career, still lingering in the period of childhood. I repeat, I am glad this is so. There is hope in the thought, and hope is much needed, under the dark clouds which lower above the horizon. The eye of the reformer is met with angry flashes, portending disastrous times; but his heart may well beat lighter at the thought that America is young, and that she is still in the impressible stage of her existence. May he not hope that high lessons of wisdom, of justice and of truth, will yet give direction to her destiny? Were the nation older, the patriot's heart might be sadder, and the reformer's brow heavier. Its future might be shrouded in gloom, and the hope of its prophets go out in sorrow. There is consolation in the thought, that America is young....

Fellow Citizens, I am not wanting in respect for the fathers of this republic. The signers of the Declaration of Independence were brave men. They were great men too—great enough to give fame to a great age. It does not often happen to a nation to raise, at one time, such a number of truly great men. The point from which I am compelled to view them is not, certainly, the most favorable; and yet I cannot contemplate their great deeds with less than admiration. They were statesmen, patriots and heroes, and for the good they did, and the principles they contended for, I will unite with you to honor their memory....

Friends and citizens, I need not enter further into the causes which led to this anniversary. Many of you understand them better than I do. You could instruct me in regard to them. That is a branch of knowledge in which you feel, perhaps, a much deeper interest than your speaker. The causes which led to the separation of the colonies from the British crown have never lacked for a tongue. They have all been taught in your common schools, narrated at your firesides, unfolded from your pulpits, and thundered from your legislative halls, and are as familiar to you as household words. They form the staple of your national poetry and eloquence....

My business, if I have any here today, is with the present. The accepted time with God and his cause is the ever-living now....

Fellow-citizens, pardon me, allow me to ask, why am I called upon to speak here today? What have I, or those I represent, to do with your national independence? Are the great principles of political freedom and of natural justice, embodied in that Declaration of Independence, extended to us? and am I, therefore, called upon to bring our humble offering to the national altar, and to confess the benefits and express devout gratitude for the blessings resulting from your independence to us?

Would to God, both for your sakes and ours, that an affirmative answer could be truthfully returned to these questions! Then would my task be light, and my burden easy and delightful. For *who* is there so cold, that a nation's sympathy could not warm him? Who so obdurate and dead to the claims of gratitude, that would not thankfully acknowledge such priceless benefits? Who so stolid and selfish, that would not give his voice to swell the hallelujahs of a nation's jubilee, when the chains of servitude had been torn from his limbs? I am not that man. In a case like that, the dumb might eloquently speak, and the "lame man leap as an hart."

But, such is not the state of the case. I say it with a sad sense of the disparity between us. I am not included within the pale of this glorious anniversary! Your high independence only reveals the immeasurable distance between us. The blessings in which you, this day, rejoice, are not enjoyed in common.—The rich inheritance of justice, liberty, prosperity and independence, bequeathed by your fathers, is shared by you, not by me. The sunlight that brought life and healing to you, has brought stripes and death to me. This Fourth July is *yours*, not *mine*. *You* may rejoice, *I* must mourn. To drag a man in fetters into the grand illuminated temple of liberty, and call upon him to join you in joyous anthems, were inhuman mockery and sacrilegious irony. Do you mean, citizens, to mock me, by asking me to speak to-day? If so, there is a parallel to your conduct. And let me warn you that it is dangerous to copy the example of a nation whose crimes, towering up to heaven, were thrown down by the breath of the Almighty, burying that nation in irrecoverable ruin! I can to-day take up the plaintive lament of a peeled and woe-smitten people! . . .

Fellow citizens; above your national, tumultuous joy, I hear the mournful wail of millions! whose chains, heavy and grievous yesterday, are, to-day, rendered more intolerable by the jubilee shouts that reach them. If I do forget, if I do not faithfully remember those bleeding children of sorrow this day, "may my right hand forget her cunning, and may my tongue cleave to the roof of my mouth!" To forget them, to pass lightly over their wrongs, and to chime in with the popular theme, would be treason most scandalous and shocking, and would make me a reproach before God and the world. My subject, then, fellow-citizens, is AMERICAN SLAVERY. I shall see, this day, and its popular characteristics, from the slave's point of view. Standing, there, identified with the American bondman, making his wrongs mine, I do not hesitate to declare, with all my soul, that the character and conduct of this nation never looked blacker to me than on this 4th of July! Whether we turn to the declarations of the past, or to the professions of the present, the conduct of the nation seems equally hideous and revolting. America is false to the past, false to the present, and solemnly binds herself to be false to the future. Standing with God and the crushed and bleeding slave on this occasion, I will, in the name of humanity which is outraged, in the name of liberty which is fettered, in the name of the constitution and the Bible, which are disregarded and trampled upon, dare to call in question and to denounce, with all the emphasis I can command, everything that serves to perpetuate slavery—the great sin and shame of America! "I will not equivocate; I will not excuse;" I will use the severest language I can command; and yet not one word shall escape me that any man, whose judgment is not blinded by prejudice, or who is not at heart a slaveholder, shall not confess to be right and just.

. . . What point in the anti-slavery creed would you have me argue? On what branch of the subject do the people of this country need light? Must I undertake to prove that the slave is a man? That point is conceded already. Nobody doubts it. The slaveholders themselves acknowledge it in the enactment of laws for their government. They acknowledge it when they punish disobedience on the part of the slave. There are seventy-two crimes in the State of Virginia, which, if committed by a black man (no matter how ignorant he be), subject him to the punishment of death; while only two of the same crimes will subject a white man to the like punishment. What is this but the acknowledgement that the slave is a moral, intellectual and responsible being. The manhood of the slave is conceded. It is admitted in the fact that Southern statute books are covered with enactments forbidding, under severe fines and penalties, the teaching of the slave to read or to write. When you can point to any such laws, in reference to the beasts of the field, then I may consent to argue the manhood of the slave. . . .

Would you have me argue that man is entitled to liberty? that he is the rightful owner of his own body? You have already declared it. Must I argue the wrongfulness of slavery? Is that a question for Republicans? Is it to be settled by the rules of logic and argumentation, as a matter beset with great difficulty, involving a doubtful application of the principle of justice, hard to be understood? How should I look to-day, in the presence of Americans, dividing, and subdividing a discourse, to show that men have a natural right to freedom? speaking of it relatively, and positively, negatively, and affirmatively. To do so, would be to make myself ridiculous, and to offer an insult to your understanding. -There is not a man beneath the canopy of heaven, that does not know that slavery is wrong *for him*.

What, am I to argue that it is wrong to make men brutes, to rob them of their liberty, to work them without wages, to keep them ignorant of their relations to their fellow men, to beat them with sticks, to flay their flesh with the lash, to load their limbs with irons, to hunt them with dogs, to sell them at auction, to sunder their families, to knock out their teeth, to burn their flesh, to starve them into obedience and submission to their masters? Must I argue that a system thus marked with blood, and stained with pollution, is *wrong* [!] No! I will not. I have better employment for my time and strength than such arguments would imply.

What, then, remains to be argued? Is it that slavery is not divine; that God did not establish it; that our doctors of divinity are mistaken? There is blasphemy in the thought. That which is inhuman, cannot be divine! *Who* can reason on such a proposition? They that can, may; I cannot. The time for such argument is past.

At a time like this, scorching irony, not convincing argument, is needed. O! had I the ability, and could I reach the nation's ear, I would, to day, pour out a fiery stream of biting ridicule, blasting reproach, withering sarcasm, and stern rebuke. For it is not light that is needed, but fire; it is not the gentle shower, but thunder. We need the storm, the whirlwind, and the earthquake. The feeling of the nation must be quickened; the conscience of the nation must be roused; the propriety of the nation must be startled; the hypocrisy of the nation must be exposed; and its crimes against God and man must be proclaimed and denounced.

What, to the American slave, is your 4th of July? I answer: a day that reveals to him, more than all other days in the year, the gross injustice and cruelty to which he is the constant victim. To him, your celebration is a sham; your boasted liberty, an unholy license; your national greatness, swelling vanity; your sounds of rejoicing are empty and heartless; your denunciations of tyrants, brass fronted impudence; your shouts of liberty and equality, hollow mockery; your prayers and hymns, your sermons and thanksgivings, with all your religious parade, and solemnity, are, to him, mere bombast, fraud, deception, impiety, and hypocrisy—a thin veil to cover up crimes which would disgrace a nation of savages. There is not a nation on the earth guilty of practices, more shocking and bloody, than are the people of these United States, at this very hour.

Go where you may, search where you will, roam through all the monarchies and despotisms of the old world, travel through South America, search out every abuse, and when you have found the last, lay your facts by the side of the everyday practices of this nation, and you will say with me, that, for revolting barbarity and shameless hypocrisy, America reigns without a rival . . .

Allow me to say, in conclusion, notwithstanding the dark picture I have this day presented of the state of the nation, I do not despair of this country. There are forces in operation, which must inevitably work the downfall of slavery. "The arm of the Lord is not shortened," and the doom of slavery is certain.

Questions for Discussion

1. Douglass finds solace in the United States being "young" and "in the impressionable stage of her existence." Is this a useful framework for understanding a nation's sociopolitical landscape?
2. How democratic is the nation that Douglass describes? Why are his abolitionist views a minority position at the time?
3. What did Douglass mean when he declared that "O! had I the ability, and could I reach the nation's ear, I would, to day, pour out a fiery stream of biting ridicule, blasting reproach, withering sarcasm, and stern rebuke. For it is not light that is needed, but fire; it is not the gentle shower, but thunder. We need the storm, the whirlwind, and the earthquake."
4. How do Douglass's words connect with the Constitution? That document obliquely approaches the subject of slavery. Is the Constitution ultimately proslavery, antislavery, or neutral on the issue?
5. What is the Fourth of July's relevance in the present day?
6. We are over one hundred and seventy years past Douglass's speech. How has the United States fared with the issues that he raised that summer day in Rochester?

Further Reading

Brewster, Francis E. *Slavery and the Constitution. Both Sides of the Question.* n.p., 1850.

Douglass, Frederick. "Our Composite Nationality." *The Speeches of Frederick Douglass: A Critical Edition*, edited by John R. Mckivigan, Julie Husband, and Heather L. Kaufman. Yale University Press, 2018.

Douglass, Frederick. "The Slaveholders' Rebellion." *Frederick Douglass: Selected Speeches and Writings*, edited by Philip S. Foner. Lawrence Hill Books, 1950.

Douglass, Frederick. "Woman and the Ballot." *Treacherous Texts: U.S. Suffrage Literature, 1846–1946*, edited by Mary Chapman and Angela Mills. Rutgers University Press, 2011.

Scott v. Sandford, 60 U.S. 393 (1856). [See opinion by Curtis.]

Notes

1. Douglass, *Narrative of the Life of Frederick Douglass*, 21, 111, 550–551, 706–711; Holland, *Frederick Douglass: The Colored Orator*, 320–323.

2. Douglass gave another Fourth of July speech during the second year of the Civil War in Yates County, New York. There he very somberly situated the war's origins in the Southern defense of slavery, called on the federal government to make use of Black soldiers, criticized George B. McClellan's military aptitude, and called for the abolition of slavery. See Douglass, "The Slaveholders' Rebellion."

The emancipation of the negroes, January 1863 - The past and the future.
(Drawn by Mr. Thomas Nast, Library of Congress.)

10

Emancipation Proclamation (1862)

Abraham Lincoln

Introduction

Decades of turmoil over the institution of slavery climaxed with the 1860 election of Abraham Lincoln as President of the United States. Lincoln, a Republican candidate, supported the non-extension of slavery and had spoken in his House Divided Speech of 1858 that he believed "this government cannot endure permanently, half slave, and half free." Seven slave states reacted to the election by seceding from the Union and forming a confederacy to protect slavery, with four more states joining later. The remaining states went to war to preserve the Union.

Despite Lincoln's opposition to slavery, he hesitated to make it a war aim. He needed to retain support in the Border States—slave states that stayed in the Union— and Lincoln withstood pressure from abolitionists to strengthen his hold over this region.

By mid-1862, however, the dynamics of the war had forced changes. Slaves fled to Union lines, and by international practice, those who had worked on behalf of the Confederate military were subject to seizure as contraband of war in the First Confiscation Act in 1861. Soon slaves entered Union lines with families in tow. Many Federal officers refused to send the family back into slavery, and by 1862 the War Department forbade soldiers from assisting in the return of fugitive slaves. Slavery was slowly eroding.

Meanwhile, the Union suffered disastrous losses with modest results. Enlistments slowed to a trickle as the Northern public became disenchanted with the war's progress. The Republican-controlled Congress and Lincoln had to strengthen the war effort. In mid-July 1862, Congress passed both the Second Confiscation Act, authorizing the seizure of property, including slaves, of those in rebellion against the Union, and the Militia Act, permitting the president to utilize Blacks "for any military or naval service for which they may be found competent." Five days later Lincoln circulated the Emancipation Proclamation to his cabinet for consideration. Lincoln needed to employ the single greatest untapped resource, African Americans, for the Federal cause, stripping laborers from the Rebels and using them as laborers and soldiers for the Union. One cabinet member convinced Lincoln to delay until the next Union battlefield victory to issue it from a position of strength.

Not until September 22, 1862, after the victory at Antietam, did Lincoln issue the Preliminary Emancipation Proclamation. The document sought support for compensated emancipation for areas that the Union forces occupied, and it liberated all slaves in areas that Federal authorities did not control by January 1, 1863. He delayed the enforcement in case states that were in rebellion returned to the Union. In effect, the Proclamation freed no one, but it pledged that as Union armies advanced and slaves fled to its lines, they would liberate slaves, and those slaves would be forever free. It was now a war for reunion *and* abolitionism.

Initially, both Proclamations generated mixed sentiments. While abolitionists applauded them, as did people who sought to end the war rapidly and punish slaveholders for causing an unnecessary war, many others howled that they would not fight or support a war to free slaves. Yet over time most northerners agreed with Lincoln that slavery must be destroyed for a true reunion of the states.

In 1865, the people adopted the Thirteenth Amendment to the U.S. Constitution, abolishing slavery.—Joseph T. Glatthaar

By the President of the United States of America:

A Proclamation.

Whereas, on the twenty-second day of September, in the year of our Lord one thousand eight hundred and sixty-two, a proclamation was issued by the President of the United States, containing, among other things, the following, to wit:

"That on the first day of January, in the year of our Lord one thousand eight hundred and sixty-three, all persons held as slaves within any State or designated part of a State, the people whereof shall then be in rebellion against the United States, shall be then, thenceforward, and forever free; and the Executive Government of the United States, including the military and naval authority thereof, will recognize and maintain the freedom of such persons, and will do no act or acts to repress such persons, or any of them, in any efforts they may make for their actual freedom.

"That the Executive will, on the first day of January aforesaid, by proclamation, designate the States and parts of States, if any, in which the people thereof, respectively, shall then be in rebellion against the United States; and the fact that any State, or the people thereof, shall on that day be, in good faith, represented in the Congress of the United States by members chosen thereto at elections wherein a majority of the qualified voters of such State shall have participated, shall, in the absence of strong countervailing testimony, be deemed conclusive evidence that such State, and the people thereof, are not then in rebellion against the United States."

Now, therefore I, Abraham Lincoln, President of the United States, by virtue of the power in me vested as Commander-in-Chief, of the Army and Navy of the United States in time of actual armed rebellion against the authority and government of the United States, and as a fit and necessary war measure for suppressing said rebellion, do, on this first day of January, in the year of our Lord one thousand eight hundred and sixty-three, and in accordance with my purpose so to do publicly proclaimed for the full period of one hundred days, from the day first above mentioned, order and designate as the States and parts of States wherein the people thereof respectively, are this day in rebellion against the United States, the following, to wit:

Arkansas, Texas, Louisiana, (except the Parishes of St. Bernard, Plaquemines, Jefferson, St. John, St. Charles, St. James Ascension, Assumption, Terrebonne, Lafourche, St. Mary, St. Martin, and Orleans, including the City of New Orleans) Mississippi, Alabama, Florida, Georgia, South Carolina, North Carolina, and Virginia, (except the forty-eight counties designated as West Virginia, and also the counties of Berkley, Accomac, Northampton, Elizabeth City, York, Princess Ann, and Norfolk, including the cities of Norfolk and Portsmouth[)], and which excepted parts, are for the present, left precisely as if this proclamation were not issued.

And by virtue of the power, and for the purpose aforesaid, I do order and declare that all persons held as slaves within said designated States, and parts of States, are, and henceforward shall be free; and that the Executive government of the United States, including the military and naval authorities thereof, will recognize and maintain the freedom of said persons.

And I hereby enjoin upon the people so declared to be free to abstain from all violence, unless in necessary self-defence; and I recommend to them that, in all cases when allowed, they labor faithfully for reasonable wages.

And I further declare and make known, that such persons of suitable condition, will be received into the armed service of the United States to garrison forts, positions, stations, and other places, and to man vessels of all sorts in said service.

And upon this act, sincerely believed to be an act of justice, warranted by the Constitution, upon military necessity, I invoke the considerate judgment of mankind, and the gracious favor of Almighty God.

In witness whereof, I have hereunto set my hand and caused the seal of the United States to be affixed.

Done at the City of Washington, this first day of January, in the year of our Lord one thousand eight hundred and sixty three, and of the Independence of the United States of America the eighty-seventh.

By the President: ABRAHAM LINCOLN
WILLIAM H. SEWARD, Secretary of State.

Questions for Discussion

1. If the cause of the war was secession, and slavery prompted secession, why did the Union not adopt efforts to destroy slavery sooner?
2. Why did Lincoln justify his Emancipation Proclamation on his power as commander-in-chief during a rebellion?
3. How did the Emancipation Proclamation enable the Union war effort to exploit the single greatest untapped resource available, African Americans?
4. Why was the destruction of slavery so vital for the restoration of the Union?
5. Based on your study of the Declaration of Independence and the Constitution, how did the Emancipation Proclamation and the abolition of slavery change the concept of liberty?

Further Reading

Franklin, John Hope. *The Emancipation Proclamation*. Wiley-Blackwell, 1994.
Guelzo, Allen C. *Lincoln's Emancipation Proclamation: The End of Slavery in America*. Simon & Schuster, 2006.

Holtzer, Harold. *Emancipating Lincoln: The Proclamation in Text, Context, and Memory*. Harvard University Press, 2012.

McPherson, James M. *Battle Cry of Freedom: The Civil War Era*. Oxford University Press, 1988.

Oakes, James. *Freedom National: The Destruction of Slavery in the United States, 1861–1865*. W. W. Norton, 2013.

FRANK LESLIE'S ILLUSTRATED NEWSPAPER.

MENDING THE FAMILY KETTLE.

COLUMBIA—"*Now, Andy, I wish you and your boys would hurry up that job, because I want to use that kettle right away. You are all talking too much about it.*"

UNION ADAMS,
HOSIER, GLOVER,
AND
SHIRT MAKER,
No. 637 BROADWAY,
NEW YORK CITY. tfo

MAGIC LANTERN
AND
Stereoscope.
We are now receiving the most comprehensive and finest importation of glass views ever made to America,

REMOVAL.
BROADWAY RUBBER EMPORIUM.
SHIFFER & CO.,
Have removed from their old store to
No. 713 BROADWAY,
Corner below New York Hotel. A large and complete assortment of
VULCANITE JEWELRY,
" INDIA RUBBER
and Fancy Goods.
o 713 BROADWAY.

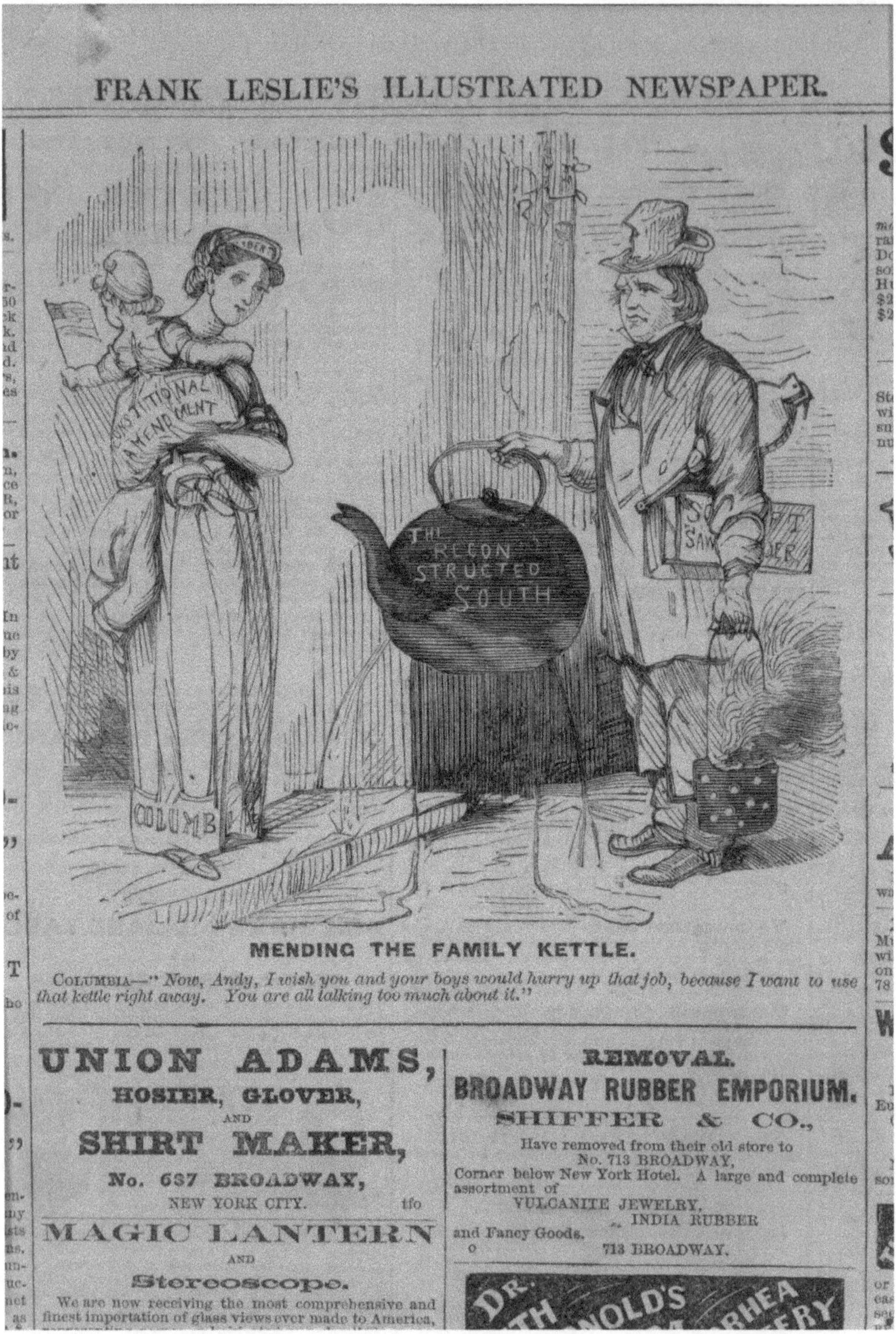

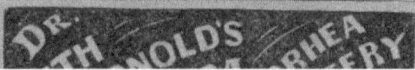

In June 1866 Frank Leslie's Illustrated Newspaper depicted President Andrew Johnson holding a leaking kettle, labeled, "The Reconstructed South," and Columbia, a woman holding a baby representing the 14th Amendment. The caption conveys Columbia's impatience with Johnson's policies to restore the Union and her intent to enforce the 14th Amendment as quickly as possible. (Library of Congress)

11

The Fourteenth Amendment (1868)

John A. Bingham and others

Introduction

On May 8, 1866, Congressman Thaddeus Stevens explained the import of the Fourteenth Amendment in a speech to the U.S. House of Representatives. The proposed amendment, he affirmed, would ensure that "the law which operates upon one man shall operate equally upon all." He stressed, "Whatever law protects the white man shall afford 'equal protection' to the black man."

While its aim was simple, the amendment itself was sweeping in its impact. No amendment to the Constitution has been the pretext for more litigation than the Fourteenth Amendment. Certainly, no other amendment has been more central to the expansion of federal power and the rights of citizens.

Like the Thirteenth and Fifteenth Amendments that were adopted after the Civil War, the Fourteenth Amendment addressed issues related to formerly enslaved Americans. The Thirteenth Amendment had abolished slavery but did nothing to guarantee the civil rights of Black Americans. During 1865 and 1866, state legislatures in the former Confederacy passed laws that extended only severely limited rights for Black southerners. In response, Stevens and other northern Republicans countered with the Fourteenth Amendment.

The amendment consists of four sections. The first section, which contains only 80 words, has had the most far-reaching impact. It continues to define citizenship in the United States. It superseded the Supreme Court's decision in *Dred Scott v. Sandford* (1857), which had held that Americans descended from African slaves could not be U.S. citizens. The section establishes that citizenship in the United States is universal and that citizenship extends to everyone born here. Whereas previously the Bill of Rights had only constrained the federal government, the amendment prohibits states and local governments from depriving persons of life, liberty, or property without fair procedures or "due process."

The amendment aroused controversy from its inception. In the North, the legislatures in Ohio and New Jersey passed and but then rescinded their support of the amendment. It was only ratified by enough states after Congress required that the states of the defeated Confederacy ratify it in order to regain representation in Congress. Conservative white southerners bitterly opposed the amendment and resorted to violence, intimidation, and legislation to subvert its intent.

Section Two of the amendment aroused opposition among women's suffragists, including Elizabeth Cady Stanton and Susan B. Anthony because it was the only provision of the Constitution to explicitly discriminate based on sex by guaranteeing the right to vote only to men.

Subsequent interpretations of the amendment by the Supreme Court have generated controversy to the present day. The Court concluded that business corporations, which proliferated during the rise of industrial capitalism, enjoyed the same protections as individual citizens. On this basis the Court limited the power of states to regulate private contracts between workers and employers.

Ignoring the drafters' intentions during more than a half century after the amendment's ratification, the Court interpreted narrowly the guarantee of equal protection and due process for Black Americans. In *Plessy v. Ferguson* (1896) and other decisions, the Court reconciled the expansion of racial discrimination (segregation) with the Fourteenth Amendment. Not until the 1930s and accelerating thereafter, did the Court begin to use the amendment to dismantle the legal edifice of white supremacy.

Since World War II, the amendment provided the basis for landmark Supreme Court decisions, including *Brown v. Board of Education* (1954) banning racial segregation in public schools, *Loving v. Virginia* (1967), banning prohibitions on interracial marriage; *Roe v. Wade* (1973), establishing legal abortion (overturned in 2022); *Obergefell v. Hodges* (2015), protecting the right to same-sex marriage; and *Students for Fair Admissions v. Harvard* (2023), banning race-based college admissions.

Given the sweep of the Fourteenth Amendment and its continuing relevance to many issues of the day, it is certain to remain one of the most influential and contested foundations of American democracy.—W. Fitzhugh Brundage

Section 1

All persons born or naturalized in the United States, and subject to the jurisdiction thereof, are citizens of the United States and of the State wherein they reside. No State shall make or enforce any law which shall abridge the privileges or immunities of citizens of the United States; nor shall any State deprive any person of life, liberty, or property, without due process of law; nor deny to any person within its jurisdiction the equal protection of the laws.

Section 2

Representatives shall be apportioned among the several States according to their respective numbers, counting the whole number of persons in each State, excluding Indians not taxed. But when the right to vote at any election for the choice of electors for President and Vice-President of the United States, Representatives in Congress, the Executive and Judicial officers of a State, or the members of the Legislature thereof, is denied to any of the male inhabitants of such State, being twenty-one years of age, and citizens of the United States, or in any way abridged, except for participation in rebellion, or other crime, the basis of representation therein shall be reduced in the proportion which the number of such male citizens shall bear to the whole number of male citizens twenty-one years of age in such State.

Section 3

No person shall be a Senator or Representative in Congress, or elector of President and Vice-President, or hold any office, civil or military, under the United States, or under any State, who, having previously taken an oath, as a member of Congress, or as an officer of the United States, or as a member of any State legislature, or as an executive or judicial officer of any State, to support the Constitution of the United States, shall have engaged in insurrection or rebellion against the same, or given aid or comfort to the enemies thereof. But Congress may by a vote of two-thirds of each House, remove such disability.

Section 4

The validity of the public debt of the United States, authorized by law, including debts incurred for payment of pensions and bounties for services in suppressing insurrection or rebellion, shall not be questioned. But neither the United States nor any State shall assume or pay any debt or obligation incurred in aid of insurrection or rebellion against the United States, or any claim for the loss or emancipation of any slave; but all such debts, obligations and claims shall be held illegal and void.

Section 5

The Congress shall have power to enforce, by appropriate legislation, the provisions of this article.

Questions for Discussion

1. How does the Fourteenth Amendment protect freedom?
2. What is the Citizenship Clause, and how did it change the definition of citizenship?
3. Does the Fourteenth Amendment promote equality?
4. What are some of the implications of the right to "due process of law" and "the equal protection of the laws"?
5. Why has the Fourteenth Amendment been a flashpoint for controversy since its adoption more than a century and a half ago?

Further Reading

In *The Slaughter-House Cases* (1873), the Court ruled that the Privileges or Immunities Clause of the Fourteenth Amendment only protects the legal rights that are associated with federal U.S. citizenship, not those that pertain to state citizenship.
See https://tile.loc.gov/storage-services/service/ll/usrep/usrep083/usrep083036/usrep083036.pdf

In *United States v. Wong Kim Ark* (1898), the Court held that under the Fourteenth Amendment, a man born within the United States to Chinese citizens who have a permanent domicile and residence in the United States was a citizen of the United States.
See https://tile.loc.gov/storage-services/service/ll/usrep/usrep169/usrep169649/usrep169649.pdf

In *Brown v. Mississippi* (1936), the Court banned involuntary confessions extracted by force as a violation of the Due Process Clause of the Fourteenth Amendment. See https://tile.loc.gov/storage-services/service/ll/usrep/usrep297/usrep297278/usrep297278.pdf

In *Loving v. Virginia* (1967), the Court ruled that laws banning interracial marriage violate the Equal Protection and Due Process Clauses of the Fourteenth Amendment. This decision subsequently was cited as precedent when the Court declared prohibitions on same sex marriage to be unconstitutional in *Obergefell v. Hodges* (2015). See https://tile.loc.gov/storage-services/service/ll/usrep/usrep388/usrep388001/usrep388001.pdf

For the historical context out of which the Fourteenth Amendment emerged, see Eric Foner, *The Second Founding: How the Civil War and Reconstruction Remade the Constitution* (W. W. Norton, 2020).

This graphic and text describe the Ku Klux Klan's attempted lynching of John A. Campbell in Moore County, North Carolina in August 1871. (East Carolina University Digital Collections)

12

Testimony on the Ku Klux Klan in North Carolina (1871)
Joseph G. Hester

Introduction

Racial violence was a significant factor in North Carolina politics during Reconstruction and in the 1890s. In the years after the Civil War, some North Carolinians engaged in counterrevolutionary violence to halt the nation's advance into interracial democracy. The Ku Klux Klan, which may have had a membership of 40,000 in this period, and similar organizations terrorized Black and white Republicans in an effort to reverse the war's gains.[1]

In 1894, a Fusion Party—comprised of Black and white Republicans and white Populists who were fed up with the Democrats' economic policies—defeated the state's Democrats. These Populists "placed class interests above racial solidarity" in their "working alliance" with the Republicans.[2] Lacking the numbers to take power back via politics, the conservatives launched a nearly year-long, "statewide campaign of racist appeals and political violence aimed at shattering the coalition of black Republicans and white Populists" which culminated in the 1898's Wilmington Massacre, wherein the white supremacists killed what may have been as many as two hundred and fifty Black people. As one historian argued, because they "were able to murder blacks in daylight and overthrow a legitimately elected Republican government without penalty or federal intervention" it became abundantly clear that "the white-supremacy campaign was triumphant on all fronts."[3]

The following year, North Carolina conservatives sidestepped the Fifteenth Amendment to the United States Constitution, which declared that citizens right to vote could not be "denied or abridged... on account of race, color, or previous condition of servitude." In addition to gerrymandering, the Assembly pushed for an amendment to the state constitution which added a poll tax and literacy requirement for voting. It was ratified in

August 1900, with a vote of 182,217 to 128,285. Most of the resistance came from western and central counties with small Black populations.⁴

The following document is the congressional testimony of Joseph G. Hester, a deputy United States marshal in Raleigh, who worked with several people whom the Klan attacked during Reconstruction.— Antwain K. Hunter

WASHINGTON, D. C. June 7, 1871.
JOSEPH G. HESTER sworn and examined.
By the CHAIRMAN:

Question. Where do you reside?
Answer. In Raleigh, North Carolina.
Question. How long have you lived there?
Answer. I have been living there four years.
Question. Are you a native of North Carolina?
Answer. Yes, sir; I was born in the adjoining county of Granville.
Question. State whether you have been acting there in the capacity of deputy marshal of the United States.
Answer. I have.
Question. State whether there have been, within your knowledge, whippings by men in disguise, within the last four or five months . . . and state what those cases were.
Answer. In the month of January I went to a place called Big Poplar, at the corner of Harnett, Moore, and Chatham Counties, with a warrant to arrest some parties charged with going in disguise upon the public highways, and upon the premises of William Judd, Stokes Judd, and Anderson Dickens, and of burning a church on the land of Anderson Dickens. I . . . arrested five of the parties charged in the warrant, summoned the witnesses, and carried the prisoners to Raleigh . . . The prisoners, after giving bond, went home, and also the witnesses. Two or three days afterward William Judd, who had been previously whipped, and was the complainant against the parties in the first case, came to the city of Raleigh again, and made a second complaint, that upon his return the Ku-Klux had attacked him the second time. He ran into the woods with his family. They all made their escape at that time, except a woman named Bella Douglass, who was not very well at the time . . . They caught her in the house, took her from the house . . . and whipped her severely. She only recognized one of the parties.
By Mr. POOL:

Question. Was she a white woman?

Answer. She was a colored woman. The warrant was issued for the one whom she recognized. His name was John Yerby Thomas. . . . I went after him; found him at his residence; arrested him; brought him to Raleigh, and summoned Bella Douglass and Judd as witnesses. They came down, and the case was heard. . . . While up there to arrest Thomas, a Mr. Henderson Judd, a white man of considerable knowledge and information, who loaned me a horse when I was up on the first occasion to go around and endeavor to arrest the parties, informed me that on their return there they took him away from his residence, took the guns and pistols that he had for his own defense, shot his dogs, carried him five miles from his home, and there dismounted him, and he was compelled to walk home in the night, over a very rough, rocky road. He is an old and decrepit man, some sixty-five or seventy years of age. . . .

By the CHAIRMAN:

Question. State the whole history of that transaction as it was disclosed in the testimony, the original case in which the Judds were parties.

Answer. The Judds were freedmen who formerly belonged to a gentleman named Henderson Judd. Their names was Judd. They assumed the name of their former master, as most of them do down there...

Question. What had he done for them?

Answer. When they were liberated he divided off some land for his former slaves, and told them that they had been good servants, and he desired to make some provision for them; he gave them assistance—oxen and means of cultivating the ground. They had been laboring there; they raised cotton and corn, and had accumulated some means . . . They had built them a church on the land of Anderson Dickens, who gave them an acre of land for that purpose. . . .

Question. Was Dickens a negro or a white man?

Answer. He was a white man. He was the man who gave them the ground to build them the church on, near where the Judds live—in the same neighborhood. Soon after that these disguised men, as appeared by the evidence of Mrs. Dickens and her husband, went to the house of Anderson Dickens, and with fence-rails broke down the doors of the house and went in, compelled Dickens and his wife to get up from the bed in their night-clothes, and with threats of violence compelled them to take fire from their own place and carry it to the church. There they compelled Dickens to take benches that were in the church and pile them in the middle of the floor, and compelled his wife to gather brush and sticks from the woods around and kindle the fire. The fire was kindled, and the church was soon in flames. They were ordered to go home and never mention to any living being what had happened. . . .

Question. State anything further that happened in connection with the burning of the church. . . .

Answer. . . . They went to William Judd's and whipped one of his sons; then they went to Stokes Judd's and whipped him. These were both colored men. That is about all of that case.

By the CHAIRMAN:

Question. What did they state to these persons as their purpose? Was that disclosed in the testimony?

Answer. They said they were going to drive the negroes out of the country; that they were not going to allow them to be there; that they could not be holding "jayhawking meetings" . . . I do not know what they mean by that. . . . I suppose, Union League meetings . . . The expression was that they could not be holding "jayhawking meetings" there; that they would not permit them to have the church. They burned the church down. . . .

By Mr. POOL: . . .

Question. What case came next under your observation?

Answer. The case of Essic Harris, a colored man, who lived in Chatham County, who was employed by a gentleman named Finch; his character, as given to me by Finch, was good. He had been living with him ever since the close of the war, and was an honest, industrious laborer. He had a gun in his possession, which he used for hunting purposes . . . The Ku-Klux had been in the habit of going down and taking the guns away from all colored people in that county; he said he was not afraid of them; that he had his gun and did not think he would be disturbed. Soon after that a band of some twelve or thirteen . . . went to the place where Harris lived;

just before getting to his house they passed a place where a colored man by the name of Sampson Perkins lived; they took Sampson Perkins out from his house and told him he must go with them to Essic Harris's . . . that they were going to commence another war, and they wanted all the guns in that neighborhood; that Essic had a gun; that they would have to break down the door probably, and they wanted him (Perkins) to break down the door, so that if any one was killed by Harris it would be him, and there would be one more radical out of the way. . . . When they got to the house, they told him to go to the wood-pile and get an ax and break the door down. Just at that time, Mr. Finch, the owner of the place, heard them, and came down and begged them to go away. They threw a rock at him and told him to go back into his house and mind his own business. While their attention was attracted by Finch, Perkins ran away . . . A man by the name of Clark then took the ax in his hand; at least the captain of the company . . . commanded Clark to take the ax and break down the door, saying that he was a young recruit and had to do the dirtiest work. Clark took the ax and began to hammer against the door with it, and finally succeeded in breaking the door open. . . . Harris discharged his gun, fired a load of shot into Clark's breast. Clark fell and exclaimed that he was shot; the rest of the company picked him up and carried him off. Harris went out and called Mr. Finch from his house and told him what had happened, saying that if any one was found shot, he was the man who had done it; he carried his shot-gourd and poured some of the shot out in his hand and said, "These are the kind that were in the gun; among these," he said, "were some other shot, big shot; and if a man is found with holes in him, there will be some larger holes than the others."
By Mr. POOL: . . .

Question. Is Mr. Finch a white man?
Answer. Yes, sir; he is a white man, and belongs to the conservative party, as he stated to me.
Question. The democratic party?
Answer. Yes, sir; some of them call it the conservative party, and some of them call it the democratic party.
By the CHAIRMAN:

Question. Please proceed with your statement.

Answer. On the application of Harris a warrant was issued . . . There were seven persons named in that warrant . . . I went to the neighborhood of Harris and succeeded in arresting six of the persons. . . . On inquiring if any doctor had been along the road where I expected Clark lived, we found that a doctor had been sent for in a great hurry the very morning after this occurrence, and by that means I found where Clark was located. . . . I told him I had a warrant for him. . . . Clark at first stated that he was unable to travel and could not go with me; that it would kill him to have to ride in a wagon. I told him I should have to take him, dead or alive. He said, "Are you in earnest? Are you going to take me sure enough?" I told him, "Yes." "Well, then," said he, "I may as well get up and go." He got up . . . took out a little flask of brandy, put it in his pocket, put on his coat, and got in the wagon. I did not hear him complain at all during the whole ride from there to Raleigh.

Question: Was he wounded?

Answer: . . . the shot had been picked out; there was a little sore on his breast, but nothing that prevented him from traveling. . . .

Question: Did you examine the wound?

Answer: Yes, sir: I opened his shirt-bosom and looked at it. . . . The wound seemed to have been made by very small shot, with the exception of three or four holes which were evidently made by larger shot. . . .

By the CHAIRMAN:

Question. Do you know of any more recent case than that of Harris?

Answer. Yes, sir. . . The case in Rutherford and Cleveland Counties, a couple of weeks ago. The parties were charged with going upon the public highways in disguise, and upon the premises of *Aaron V. Biggerstaff*, whipping him and abusing his family. . . . In this case there were thirty names in the warrant. I asked General Morgan to let me have a small detachment of troops. He gave me a sergeant and nine men. I arrested the parties, all but two . . . and carried them to Shelby, the county-seat of Cleveland County . . . I told him the witnesses had been summoned and would be in town early the next morning. I got there in the afternoon. Next morning the witnesses did not come, and we had no evidence against the prisoners. Later in the day we ascertained from different persons who had come in from that section of the country that the witnesses had been attacked while camped out some ten miles from Shelby. . . .

Question. Attacked by whom?

Answer. Attacked by a band of disguised men. Biggerstaff was taken out and whipped severely, beaten, and threatened that he would be killed if he ever informed on any one of the party. He was ordered to return back home . . .

Question. Are the portions of North Carolina in which these occurrences have recently taken place the same as those in which similar occurrences took place before? Had there been other occurrences of the kind in the counties you have named—Moore, Harnett, and Cleveland?

Answer. When I was up there to arrest the parties I have named, there were numbers of persons, both colored and white, who came to me from different sections of the country around there. They had heard I was in the neighborhood. Some showed me bruises where they had been whipped; others told me they had been driven from schools where they had been teaching colored persons, and were not permitted to teach the schools any longer.

Question. What name is given to the organization of disguised persons in that part of the State?

Answer. I have been in the habit of calling them Ku-Klux; some of them say the name is White Brotherhood, and others, Invisible Empire. I have heard different names for them. They themselves say . . . that they are not human beings . . . that they have been seven years in the bone-yards at Richmond, and have come for vengeance.

Question. From what you have observed of recent proceedings, is that organization still in existence and operation there?

Answer. I think, sir, it is on the increase. From observations and information received from different sources I think they are reorganizing all the time. I think they have changed their *modus operandi* since some of the developments have been made. . . .

Question. In the part of the State of which you speak, are persons at liberty to express their political sentiments with freedom and immunity from danger?

Answer. Those with whom I have conversed say they are not; they would be in great danger if they should get up and make a political speech, and express sentiments as republicans. . . .

Question. Did the men who were arrested state to you what their politics were?

Answer. Yes, sir; they said they belonged to the conservative democratic party. . . .

Question. What were the politics of these persons who were whipped?

Answer. They were republicans. They said they voted for General Grant in the last campaign, and one of them mentioned that when he was being whipped he was told he was whipped because he voted for Grant.

Question. When in the neighborhood where the offenses were committed, did you hear any other reason assigned for the punishment of these men; any charge made against them morally or personally?

Answer. No, sir; I heard nothing except that Stokes Judd said that one of the men who helped to whip him owed him some money; he had asked for it two or three times, and he would not pay it. They mentioned that to him in the course of whipping him, and also his voting for Grant. . . .

Question. What did you find to be the state of things there [in Cleveland, Rutherford, and Gaston Counties]? Was there a feeling of alarm in consequence of these occurrences?

Answer. Yes, sir; they seemed to be very much alarmed and uneasy, even people who lived at the county-seat in Rutherford County. One of them, a member of the present legislature of North Carolina, Mr. Justice, said that he and Mr. Carpenter, editor of a republican paper there, had been compelled, as they regarded it, for safety's sake, to keep watch at night for weeks.

Question. To what extent does that feeling prevail in the State, so far as you have had opportunities of observing?

Answer. Well, sir, my observation leads me to believe that it extends over the counties of Harnett, Moore, Chatham, Randolph, Gaston, Cleveland, Rutherford, and McDowell. I have heard of occurrences in other counties; but I have not been in other counties on any official duty in this particular. . . .

Questions for Discussion

1. What does Hester's depiction of these western North Carolina counties tell us about the intersections of politics, community, and family in the region during Reconstruction?
2. According to Hester's testimony, what were the Ku Klux Klan's goals, and how did they seek to achieve them? Who were their targets? How effective was Hester, as a federal law enforcement officer, in halting these terrorists?
3. Hester mentions firearms at various points. What role do they play in this story?
4. What does this violent aftermath of the Civil War tell us about democracy's limitations in North Carolina?

Further Reading

"Explanation of the Amendment." *The Observer* (Fayetteville, NC), April 1, 1899.
"Instructions to Red Shirts in South Carolina, 1876." In *Major Problems in the History of the American South, Volume II: The New South*, edited by Paul D. Escott and David R. Goldfield. D. C. Heath and Company, 1990.
Jennet, Norman Ethre. "The Vampire that Hovers Over North Carolina," *News and Observer*, September 27, 1898.
United States Congress. Testimony taken by the Joint Select Committee to Inquire into the Condition of Affairs in the Late Insurrectionary States. North Carolina (Washington, DC: Government Printing Office, 1872).
"White Supremacy Made Permanent." *The Observer* (Fayetteville, NC), April 1, 1899.

Notes

1. William S. Powell, *North Carolina through Four Centuries* (UNC Press, 1989), 397.
2. Leon Prather, Sr., *We Have Taken a City: The Wilmington Racial Massacre and Coup of 1898* (Fairleigh Dickinson University Press, 1984), 34–35, 51–54, 57; Leon Prather, Sr., "We Have Taken a City: A Centennial Essay," in *Democracy Betrayed: The Wilmington Race Riot of 1898 and Its Legacy*, ed. David. S. Cecelski and Timothy B. Tyson (UNC Press, 1998), 18.
3. Cecelski and Tyson, *Democracy Betrayed*; LeRae S. Umfleet, *A Day of Blood: The 1898 Wilmington Race Riot* (Raleigh, 2009), xix, 113–119.
4. United States Constitution, amend 15, sec 1; Prather, *We Have Taken a City*, 31; Powell, *North Carolina through Four Centuries*, 438.

PART THREE

THE GOSPEL OF FREEDOM

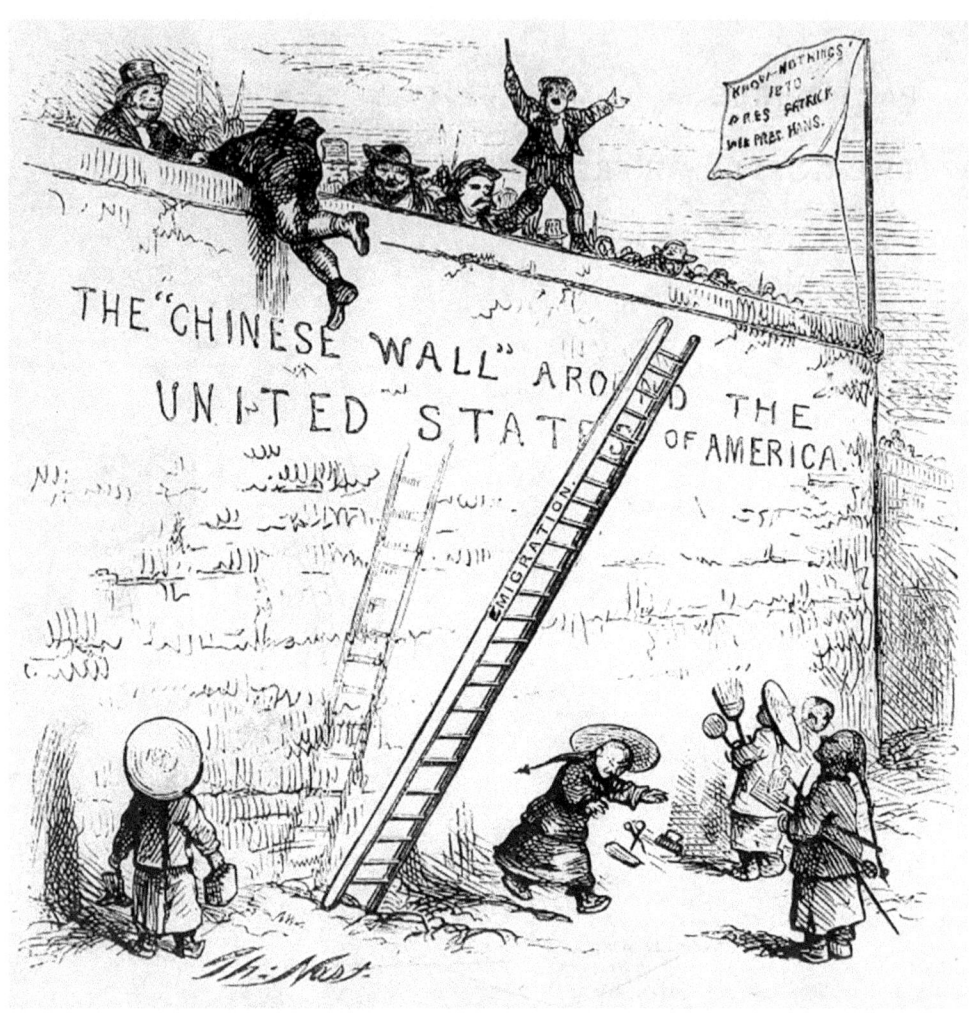

Thomas Nast, "Throwing Down the Ladder by Which They Rose," (Harper's Weekly, July 23, 1870.)

13

Chinese Exclusion Act (1882)

United States Congress

Introduction

The United States proclaims itself a nation of immigrants, yet its history of restrictive immigration policy unsettles this vision. The Act of May 6, 1882—better known as the Chinese Exclusion Act—was the first federal law to single out a specific foreign-born population for restriction. It barred Chinese laborers from entering the United States for ten years, a prohibition that was repeatedly renewed and expanded through subsequent legislation. The act also denied Chinese migrants the right to naturalize. While no other federal law explicitly barred an immigrant group from naturalization, the U.S. Supreme Court would later rule that all Asians were ineligible for citizenship, a precedent that would effectively prevent their immigration too.

At the behest of the Chinese government, however, the act also allowed Chinese laborers already living in the country to travel and return. This exemption reflected a theory of federal power that framed immigration as diplomacy rather than domestic policy. The Burlingame Treaty (1868), negotiated amid Reconstruction, promoted the free movement of Chinese migrants to the United States, enshrining the belief among policymakers that such mobility was essential to economic ties between the two nations. These two competing impulses—one driven by international relations, the other by racial exclusion—were inherently at odds, setting off legal battles over the meaning of federal power that would unfold for years.

When the steamship *S.S. Belgic* arrived in San Francisco, it carried Chae Chan Ping, a longtime U.S. resident barred from reentry under a new amendment to the 1882 act. Like many others, Chae challenged his detention through a writ of habeas corpus—Latin for "you should have the body"—which allows individuals to demand legal justification for their confinement before a court. The framers of the U.S. Constitution recognized habeas corpus as a fundamental safeguard against arbitrary detention, enshrining it in Article I, Section 9, Clause 2, ensuring that no person could be deprived of liberty without due process. Yet, to opponents of Chinese migration, its use by Chinese litigants was not a constitutional right but a manipulation of the legal system, fueling their calls for harsher administrative action.

In ruling against Chae Chan Ping, the Supreme Court declared that Congress's power to exclude noncitizens was an inherent right of national sovereignty, overriding treaties and prior legal guarantees. The decision recast immigration as a domestic issue, making policy vulnerable to political factions intent on reshaping the nation's demographics through exclusion and expulsion. It initiated a legal trajectory in which the judiciary steadily withdrew from immigration matters, granting executive administrators increasing authority. Over time, this expansive power eroded the protections for U.S. citizens, laying the groundwork for their rights to be questioned, denied, or revoked. This momentum culminated in *United States v. Ju Toy* (1905), where the justices ruled that administrative hearings alone were sufficient to determine citizenship claims, stripping U.S. citizens of the right to habeas corpus.—Heather Ruth Lee

An Act to execute certain treaty stipulations relating to Chinese.

Whereas in the opinion of the Government of the United States the coming of Chinese laborers to this country endangers the good order of certain localities within the territory thereof: Therefore,

Be it enacted by the Senate and House of Representatives of the United States of America in Congress assembled, That from and after the expiration of ninety days next after the passage of this act, and until the expiration of ten years next after the passage of this act, the coming of Chinese laborers to the United States be, and the same is hereby, suspended; and during such suspension it shall not be lawful for any Chinese laborer to come, or having so come after the expiration of said ninety days to remain within the United States.

SEC. 2. That the master of any vessel who shall knowingly bring within the United States on such vessel, and land or permit to be landed, any Chinese laborer, from any foreign port or place, shall be deemed guilty of a misdemeanor, and on conviction thereof shall be punished by a fine of not more than five hundred dollars for each and every such Chinese laborer so brought, and maybe also imprisoned for a term not exceeding one year.

SEC. 3. That the two foregoing sections shall not apply to Chinese laborers who were in the United States on the seventeenth day of November, eighteen hundred and eighty, or who shall have come into the same before the expiration of ninety days next after the passage of this act, and who shall produce to such master before going on board such vessel, and shall produce to the collector of the port in the United States at which such vessel shall arrive, the evidence hereinafter in this act required of his being one of the laborers in this section mentioned; nor shall the two foregoing sections apply to the case of any master whose vessel, being bound to a port not within the United States, shall come within the jurisdiction of the United States by reason of being in distress or in stress of weather, or touching at any port of the United States on its voyage to any foreign port or place: Provided, That all Chinese laborers brought on such vessel shall depart with the vessel on leaving port.

SEC. 4. That for the purpose of properly identifying Chinese laborers who were in the United States on the seventeenth day of November eighteen hundred and eighty, or who shall have come into the same before the expiration of ninety days next after the passage of this act, and in order to furnish them with the proper evidence of their right to go from and come to the United States of their free will and accord, as provided by the treaty between the United States and China dated November seventeenth, eighteen hundred and eighty, the collector of customs of the district from which any such Chinese laborer shall depart from the United States shall, in person or by deputy, go on board each vessel having on board any such Chinese laborers and cleared or about to sail from his district for a foreign port, and on such vessel make a list of all such Chinese laborers, which shall be entered in registry-books to be kept for that purpose, in which shall be stated the name, age, occupation, last place of residence, physical marks of peculiarities, and all facts necessary for the identification of each of such Chinese laborers, which books shall be safely kept in the custom-house.; and every such Chinese laborer so departing from the United States shall be entitled to, and shall receive, free of any charge or cost upon application therefor, from the collector or his deputy, at the time such list is taken, a certificate, signed by the collector or his deputy and attested by his seal of office, in such form as the Secretary of the Treasury shall prescribe, which certificate shall contain a statement of the name, age, occupation, last place of residence, persona description, and facts of identification of the Chinese laborer to whom the certificate is issued, corresponding with the said list and registry in all particulars. In case any Chinese laborer after having received such certificate shall leave such vessel before her departure he shall deliver his certificate to the master of the vessel, and if such Chinese laborer shall fail to return to such vessel before her departure from port the certificate shall be delivered by the master to the collector of customs for cancellation. The certificate herein provided for shall entitle the Chinese laborer to whom the same is issued to return to and re-enter the United States upon producing and delivering the same to the collector of customs of the district at which such Chinese laborer shall seek to re-enter; and upon delivery of such certificate by such Chinese laborer to the collector of customs at the time of re-entry in the United States said collector shall cause the same to be filed in the custom-house anti duly canceled.

SEC. 5. That any Chinese laborer mentioned in section four of this act being in the United States, and desiring to depart from the United States by land, shall have the right to demand and receive, free of charge or cost, a certificate of identification similar to that provided for in section four of this act to be issued to such Chinese laborers as may desire to leave the United States by water; and it is hereby made the duty of the collector of customs of the district next adjoining the foreign country to which said Chinese laborer desires to go to issue such certificate, free of charge or cost, upon application by such Chinese laborer, and to enter the same upon registry-books to be kept by him for the purpose, as provided for in section four of this act.

SEC. 6. That in order to the faithful execution of articles one and two of the treaty in this act before mentioned, every Chinese person other than a laborer who may be entitled by said treaty and this act to come within the United States, and who shall be about to come to the United States, shall be identified as so entitled by the Chinese Government in each case, such identity to be evidenced by a certificate issued under the authority of said government, which certificate shall be in the English language or (if not in the English language) accompanied by a translation into English, stating such right to come, and which certificate shall state the name, title or official rank, if any, the age, height, and all physical peculiarities, former and present occupation or profession, and place of residence in China of the person to whom the certificate is issued and that such person is entitled, conformably to the treaty in this act mentioned to come within the United States. Such certificate shall be prima-facie evidence of the fact set forth therein, and shall be produced to the collector of customs, or his deputy, of the port in the district in the United States at which the person named therein shall arrive.

SEC. 7. That any person who shall knowingly and falsely alter or substitute any name for the name written in such certificate or forge any such certificate, or knowingly utter any forged or fraudulent certificate, or falsely personate any person named in any such certificate, shall be deemed guilty of a misdemeanor; and upon conviction thereof shall be fined in a sum not exceeding one thousand dollars, and imprisoned in a penitentiary for a term of not more than five years.

SEC. 8. That the master of any vessel arriving in the United States from any foreign port or place shall, at the same time he delivers a manifest of the cargo, and if there be no cargo, then at the time of making a report of the entry of the vessel pursuant to law, in addition to the other matter required to be reported, and before landing, or permitting to land, any Chinese passengers, deliver and report to the collector of customs of the district in which such vessels shall have arrived a separate list of all Chinese passengers taken on board his vessel at any foreign port or place, and all such passengers on board the vessel at that time. Such list shall show the names of such passengers (and if accredited officers of the Chinese Government traveling on the business of that government, or their servants, with a note of such facts), and the names and other particulars, as shown by their respective certificates; and such list shall be sworn to by the master in the manner required by law in relation to the manifest of the cargo. Any willful refusal or neglect of any such master to comply with the provisions of this section shall incur the same penalties and forfeiture as are provided for a refusal or neglect to report and deliver a manifest of the cargo.

SEC. 9. That before any Chinese passengers are landed from any such line vessel, the collector, or his deputy, shall proceed to examine such passenger, comparing the certificate with the list and with the passengers; and no passenger shall be allowed to land in the United States from such vessel in violation of law.

SEC. 10. That every vessel whose master shall knowingly violate any of the provisions of this act shall be deemed forfeited to the United States, and shall be liable to seizure and condemnation in any district of the United States into which such vessel may enter or in which she may be found.

SEC. 11. That any person who shall knowingly bring into or cause to be brought into the United States by land, or who shall knowingly aid or abet the same, or aid or abet the landing in the United States from any vessel of any Chinese person not lawfully entitled to enter the United States, shall be deemed guilty of a misdemeanor, and shall, on conviction thereof, be fined in a sum not exceeding one thousand dollars, and imprisoned for a term not exceeding one year.

SEC. 12. That no Chinese person shall be permitted to enter the United States by land without producing to the proper officer of customs the certificate in this act required of Chinese persons seeking to land from a vessel. And any Chinese person found unlawfully within the United States shall be caused to be removed therefrom to the country from whence he came, by direction of the President of the United States, and at the cost of the United States, after being brought before some justice, judge, or commissioner of a court of the United States and found to be one not lawfully entitled to be or remain in the United States.

SEC.13. That this act shall not apply to diplomatic and other officers of the Chinese Government traveling upon the business of that government, whose credentials shall be taken as equivalent to the certificate in this act mentioned, and shall exempt them and their body and house- hold servants from the provisions of this act as to other Chinese persons.

SEC. 14. That hereafter no State court or court of the United States shall admit Chinese to citizenship; and all laws in conflict with this act are hereby repealed.

SEC.15. That the words "Chinese laborers", wherever used in this act shall be construed to mean both skilled and unskilled laborers and Chinese employed in mining.

Questions for Discussion

1. What political or social forces might have influenced Congress's decision to pass this law?
2. In the preamble, the 1882 act claims that Chinese immigration "endangers the good order of certain localities." What assumptions about race, labor, and economic competition does this statement reflect?
3. How does the 1882 act balance (or fail to balance) the rights of individuals against the federal government's prerogative to control immigration?

4. What does the 1882 act reveal about Congress's ability to override international agreements, and how does the text of the Act establish a legal foundation for future immigration restrictions?
5. How does the bureaucratic system established by the 1882 act—including customs officers, certificates, registries, and vessel inspections—reflect the growing power of federal administrative agencies?

Further Reading

Blaine, James G. "Chinese Immigration to the Pacific Slope." In *Political Discussions: Legislative, Diplomatic, and Popular, 1856–1886*. Henry Bill, 1887.
Burlingame Treaty of 1868. https://www.loc.gov/resource/rbpe.23602400/?q=Burlingame+Treatyandst%3Dgallery&st=pdf&pdfPage=2
Chae Chan Ping v. United States, 130 U.S. 581 (1889).
"The Habeas Corpus Mill." *Daily Alta California*, March 6, 1888.
United States v. Ju Toy, 198 U.S. 253 (1905).
U.S. Constitution, art. 1, sec. 9, cl. 2.

A photo of Charles Eastman, also known as Ohíyesa, published between 1901 and 1903. (photograph by C. M. Bell, Washington, D.C., Library of Congress)

14

The Indian's Plea for Freedom (1919)

Charles A. Eastman (Ohiyesa)

Introduction

Today, American Indians born in the United States are U.S. citizens as well as citizens of their tribal nations. When Europeans first arrived in the Americas, of course, Indigenous Americans belonged only to their own sovereign nations. In 1832 the court case *Worcester v. Georgia* set the precedent that Native nations are "distinct, independent political communities" with the right to govern themselves. As the United States grew and surrounded Native nations in the nineteenth century, American Indians increasingly sought U.S. citizenship. For many years, Indigenous Americans were not guaranteed the ability to maintain both tribal citizenship and U.S. citizenship.

One group that fought for Native citizenship was the Society of American Indians (SAI) of which Charles Eastman was a founding member. Eastman was born in Minnesota in 1858 and fled with his family from the violence of the U.S. war against his Dakota people. He was educated at a reservation boarding school and graduated from Dartmouth College in 1887 and from medical school at Boston University in 1890. Throughout his life, Eastman witnessed many disastrous changes for Native communities, even treating the wounded in the aftermath of the Wounded Knee Massacre.

Eastman was part of a generation of American Indian intellectuals who took their boarding school education—which attempted to destroy their Native identity and culture—and utilized it to advocate for American Indian rights. In 1911, Eastman and five other prominent "red progressives" founded the SAI to advocate for economic development and "to promote citizenship among Indians and to obtain the rights thereof."[1] The group had a range of positions on why American Indians needed citizenship. Many viewed U.S. citizenship as a crucial tool, both for full participation in American life and to protect Native autonomy and self-determination. Others gravitated to a view that citizenship would hasten American Indian assimilation and reduce the need for Native nations as culturally and politically distinct polities.

As the United States joined WWI, President Woodrow Wilson spoke of the need to "make the world safe for democracy." The SAI used its magazine to highlight that thousands of Native Americans answered the call and were serving. In 1917 Arthur Parker argued that when his country and liberties were "challenged, the Indian has responded and shown himself a citizen of the world."[2] At the end of the war, Wilson promoted the expansion of democracy and protection for oppressed minorities as part of his view of a new world order.

In 1919 Congress recognized the sacrifices American Indian veterans made to preserve democracy and granted citizenship to all American Indian WWI veterans. The SAI and other reformers continued to lobby for citizenship for all American Indians and succeeded with the 1924 Citizenship Act, which granted citizenship to all Native American men and women born in the United States.[3]—Raquel Escobar

---

I believe this to be an opportune moment for the "little peoples" of the earth to plead for a better observance of their individuality and rights by the more powerful and ruling nations. For we must admit that every race, however untutored, has its ideals, its standards of right and wrong, which are sometimes nearer the Christ principle than the common standards of civilization.

Certainly under the leadership of Woodrow Wilson, we of the United States have an opportunity splendid and far reaching, which may never come again. If the coming Peace Congress will deliberate unselfishly in the interests of humanity, if we can eliminate purely national bias and suspicion, then the world's after-council must establish a new international relationship. And this new order must begin at home. The old rule, the old ambitions for world domination by discovery and conquest must forever pass.

The world is tired, sick, and exhausted by a war which has brought home to us the realization that our boasted progress is after all mainly industrial and commercial—a powerful force, to be sure, but being so unspiritual, not likely to be lasting or stable. . . . The education of the child has subordinated his higher instincts to the necessities of business. Christ has been preached in vain, since his most unmistakable and unequivocal declarations are directly opposed to our excess of material development, social injustice and the accumulation of wealth.

Now we have come to a point when we may at least hope that this tremendous machine will be used toward a better readjustment of human relationships. An Indian must admire our President for the stand he has taken. It seems we are in a position to pilot the bark of humanity into a safe harbor, if this high stand can be sustained by the allies.

When the vexed Irish question and other knotty problems come up at the peace table, we may be reminded that we too, here in America, have our race troubles. How can our nation pose as the champion of the "little peoples" until it has been fair to its own? "We, too, demand our freedom!" cry those modern Greeks, the North American Indians. Their request is not hard to grant, since it involves, no separate government or territory. All we ask is full citizenship. Why not? We offered our services and our money in this war, and more in proportion to our number and means than any other race or class of the population. Yet there are people who insist on keeping us the "wards of the Government," apparently for no other reason than to use our money and our property for their own benefit....

The first white men who came here met a friendly reception and found a most beautiful and unspoiled home. Most of them came in search of treasure for themselves or their kings. A few came in an entirely different spirit. They sought religious and political self-determination. They found it, and in their contact with the simple Indian tribes, whom they counted godless and heathen, they unconsciously and in spite of themselves absorbed enough of the Indians' culture to modify their own....

It is not generally known that practically all the basic principles of the original articles of confederation of the Thirteen States were borrowed, either unconsciously or knowingly, from the league of the Six Nations and the Sioux confederacy.[4] You may ask, how came the American eagle to reach its symbolic power? I say to you, it was a reverenced symbol for untold centuries with the American Indians. Its feathers were worn by worthy men for worthy deeds. They could not be bought nor sold.

Now every treaty with the Indians in recent times has included provision for the education of their children, and it was understood that in due time the affairs of their people should be turned over to them, and that as fast as they became able to comply with the usual requirements, they should be admitted to citizenship. In fact, the Constitution expressly excludes "Indians not taxed," therefore, as they are not foreigners, when one pays his taxes, he is a citizen. Yet there has been so much confusing legislation on this matter, that I do not believe there is a learned judge in these United States who can tell an Indian's exact status without a great deal of study, and even then he may be in doubt.

The Indian Bureau, instead of being the servant of the people and of the Indians in accordance with treaty stipulations, has grown into a petty autocracy. The whole system reminds me of the story of Two-Face in the Sioux legend. He stole a child to feed on his tender substance, sucking his blood while still living, and if any one protested, or aroused by the baby's screams, attempted a rescue, he would pat it tenderly and pretend to caress it. This fine intention of the people to develop the Indian into useful citizens has given rise to an institution which is doing them positive injury.

It is not the fault of the people in a way; not perhaps the fault of any particular administration that a soldier returning from the Marne or Chateau Thierry should still find his money and land held by the Indian Bureau. When he asks for freedom, they answer him: "Can you propose anything better than the present system?" He replies: "Is there anything better today than American citizenship?"

Who is there that has faith in the power of self-development and human initiative, that would deny this opportunity to the Indian? It is true that a few will misuse their freedom; some will fall and recover themselves; most will gain direct and useful experience. It is not fair to destroy the manhood of a race by a system which must make them more inactive, dependent and beggarly with each succeeding generation.

There are no more "wild Indians." The majority have had contact with civilization for at least forty years. They have had two generations or more of schooling. Many are nominal citizens and actual tax-payers yet have no real freedom of action. . . .

In view of all that the world has just suffered in the name of justice and a fair deal for all, we appeal to all fair-minded Americans; Is it not our due that we should call this fair land ours with you in full brotherhood? Have we not defended bravely its liberties and may we not share them? . . . We ask only to enjoy with Europe's sons the full privileges of American citizenship.

Questions for Discussion

1. Why does Eastman think that 1919 is a good time for advocating for U.S. citizenship for American Indians?

2. Eastman uses Native service in the war as one justification for granting American Indians citizenship. Why do you think he uses this argument? To whom would such an argument appeal and why?
3. Eastman points out that "the original articles of confederation of the Thirteen States were borrowed . . . from the league of the Six Nations and the Sioux confederacy." What point is he trying to make, and how does that support, or not support, his argument about Indian citizenship?
4. What issues, according to Eastman, could be addressed if American Indians had citizenship?
5. Given what you know from this document and your course, how have Indigenous Americans' relationship with the United States changed over time?
6. How do you see the concept of tribal sovereignty and self-determination influencing the debate around Native American citizenship?

Further Reading

Apess, William. "Eulogy on King Philip." 1836. https://voicesofdemocracy.umd.edu/apess-eulogy-speech-text/

McGirt v. Oklahoma, 591 U.S. ___ (2020).

Muskrat, Ruth. "Address on the North American Indian." 1927. https://ualrexhibits.org/tribalwriters/artifacts/Muskrat_AddressNorthAmericanIndian.html

Native Governance Center. "What is Tribal Sovereignty." YouTube, https://www.youtube.com/watch?v=BOYcgvEU

Nixon, Richard. "Special Message to the Congress on Indian Affairs." 1970.

Notes

1. The Society of American Indians Statement of Purpose in *The Papers of the Society of American Indians*.
2. Parker, "Why the Red Man Fights for Democracy."
3. In 1920, the Constitutional amendment giving women the right to vote was ratified.
4. Eastman's Dakota people are part of the Sioux (in the Dakota language, Oceti Sakowin).

OURS...to fight for

Freedom of Speech

Freedom of Worship

Freedom from Want

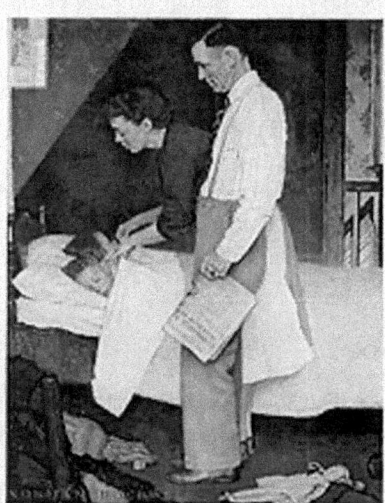

Freedom from Fear

This poster is illustrated by four paintings by Norman Rockwell for *The Saturday Evening* Post magazine's "Four Freedoms" series 1943 and thereafter the Office of War Information reprinted millions of copies. (U.S. Government Printing Office for the Office of War Information, 1943)

15

Four Freedoms (1941)

Franklin D. Roosevelt

Introduction

In November 1940 Democrat incumbent Franklin D. Roosevelt was reelected president for an unprecedented third term. With this electoral mandate, Roosevelt sought to shift his nation's public opinion regarding the expanding global war. In his State of the Union Address the following January, he proposed a new vision for sustaining the foundations of American democracy: that the security of the United States depended upon ensuring "four freedoms" for all people around the world.

This position represented a shift. During the previous decade, Americans had overwhelmingly favored isolationism in foreign affairs. Many recalled the Great War's horrific trench warfare and were appalled when subsequent evidence showed that corporations profiteered from it. The onset of the Great Depression in 1929 had also turned Americans inward, reasoning that the nation had to prioritize its domestic economic crisis. As a result, Congress passed a series of Neutrality Acts beginning in 1935 that prohibited the sale of "implements of war" and loans to belligerent nations.

President Roosevelt and some of his New Deal supporters, however, became increasingly alarmed about the spread of global fascism in Europe and Asia. He invoked the need to "quarantine the aggressor" in a 1937 speech. But reaction to the speech was so critical that Roosevelt stepped back from a more vigorous foreign policy. Only in 1939 did the president achieve a slight revision to the Neutrality Act, which allowed Western European allies a "cash and carry" program to buy U.S. arms and other goods. By June of 1940, the Nazi Army defeated France, leaving Great Britain as the only nation standing in the way of Germany's military. Thereafter, Roosevelt's Congressional allies introduced a more aggressive Lend–Lease Act that would create an "arsenal of democracy" to aid our Western European allies. This chain of events led to Roosevelt's bold "Four Freedoms" speech.

But the preservation of freedom as justification for U.S. intervention in what would become World War II came as much from grassroots social movements of the 1930s as from the federal government. In 1932 Roosevelt called for "bold, persistent experimentation" to get the nation out of the Great Depression on behalf of the "forgotten man."[1] As a result, labor unions, political and cultural activists, ethnic and racial organizations, and New Deal liberals pushed for old-age insurance, child labor laws, social security, unemployment insurance, the abolition of Jim Crow racial policies, and more. This pressure from the grassroots resulted in Second New Deal legislation that created America's first social welfare state.

The social movements of the 1930s also increasingly connected their struggles for democratic rights to parallel campaigns worldwide. By 1935, when the Communist Party called for a global popular front to abandon sectarianism and unite with anyone opposed to fascism, many Americans were already fostering those coalitions. The cumulative impact of this domestic and international activism pushed New Deal Democrats away from the negative rights of laissez-faire unregulated capitalism to endorse positive rights of freedom assured by the government. These positive rights included education, housing, health care, and a minimum standard of living. But the New Deal had its limits—especially because southern Democrats thwarted civil rights demands, exposing their own homegrown fascism.

The combination of a world crisis and the transformation of many Americans' expectations of freedom shaped the context for Roosevelt's four freedoms pronouncement. But in drafting this speech, Roosevelt added the phrase "everywhere in the world," surprising his advisors. Those advisors objected but the president stood his ground, saying, "The world is getting so small that even the people in Java are getting to be our neighbors now." Not all Americans believed in such a widespread definition of freedom. Indeed, it would take the Japanese attack on Pearl Harbor almost a year later before the United States entered the war. But Roosevelt's robust conceptualization of freedom has had a profound legacy. These freedoms defined our participation in the Second World War, propelled the subsequent formation of the United Nations, and inspired universal human rights language and campaigns for the rest of the century and beyond.—Erik S. Gellman

Mr. President, Mr. Speaker, Members of the Seventy-seventh Congress:

I address you, the Members of the Seventy-seventh Congress, at a moment unprecedented in the history of the Union. I use the word "unprecedented," because at no previous time has American security been as seriously threatened from without as it is today.

Since the permanent formation of our Government under the Constitution, in 1789, most of the periods of crisis in our history have related to our domestic affairs. Fortunately, only one of these—the four-year War Between the States—ever threatened our national unity. Today, thank God, one hundred and thirty million Americans, in forty-eight States, have forgotten points of the compass in our national unity.

It is true that prior to 1914 the United States often had been disturbed by events in other Continents. We had even engaged in two wars with European nations and in a number of undeclared wars in the West Indies, in the Mediterranean and in the Pacific for the maintenance of American rights and for the principles of peaceful commerce. But in no case had a serious threat been raised against our national safety or our continued independence. . . .

Every realist knows that the democratic way of life is at this moment being directly assailed in every part of the world—assailed either by arms, or by secret spreading of poisonous propaganda by those who seek to destroy unity and promote discord in nations that are still at peace.

During sixteen long months this assault has blotted out the whole pattern of democratic life in an appalling number of independent nations, great and small. The assailants are still on the march, threatening other nations, great and small.

Therefore, as your President, performing my constitutional duty to "give to the Congress information of the state of the Union," I find it, unhappily, necessary to report that the future and the safety of our country and of our democracy are overwhelmingly involved in events far beyond our borders.

Armed defense of democratic existence is now being gallantly waged in four continents. If that defense fails, all the population and all the resources of Europe, Asia, Africa and Australasia will be dominated by the conquerors. Let us remember that the total of those populations and their resources in those four continents greatly exceeds the sum total of the population and the resources of the whole of the Western Hemisphere—many times over.

In times like these it is immature—and incidentally, untrue—or anybody to brag that an unprepared America, single-handed, and with one hand tied behind its back, can hold off the whole world.

No realistic American can expect from a dictator's peace international generosity, or return of true independence, or world disarmament, or freedom of expression, or freedom of religion—or even good business.

Such a peace would bring no security for us or for our neighbors. "Those, who would give up essential liberty to purchase a little temporary safety, deserve neither liberty nor safety."

As a nation, we may take pride in the fact that we are softhearted; but we cannot afford to be soft-headed.

We must always be wary of those who with sounding brass and a tinkling cymbal preach the "ism" of appeasement.

We must especially beware of that small group of selfish men who would clip the wings of the American eagle in order to feather their own nests....

Certainly this is no time for any of us to stop thinking about the social and economic problems which are the root cause of the social revolution which is today a supreme factor in the world.

For there is nothing mysterious about the foundations of a healthy and strong democracy. The basic things expected by our people of their political and economic systems are simple. They are:

Equality of opportunity for youth and for others.
Jobs for those who can work.
Security for those who need it.
The ending of special privilege for the few.
The preservation of civil liberties for all.
The enjoyment of the fruits of scientific progress in a wider and constantly rising standard of living.

These are the simple, basic things that must never be lost sight of in the turmoil and unbelievable complexity of our modern world. The inner and abiding strength of our economic and political systems is dependent upon the degree to which they fulfill these expectations.

Many subjects connected with our social economy call for immediate improvement.

As examples:

We should bring more citizens under the coverage of old-age pensions and unemployment insurance.
We should widen the opportunities for adequate medical care.
We should plan a better system by which persons deserving or needing gainful employment may obtain it.
I have called for personal sacrifice. I am assured of the willingness of almost all Americans to respond to that call.

A part of the sacrifice means the payment of more money in taxes. In my Budget Message I shall recommend that a greater portion of this great defense program be paid for from taxation than we are paying today. No person should try, or be allowed, to get rich out of this program; and the principle of tax payments in accordance with ability to pay should be constantly before our eyes to guide our legislation.

If the Congress maintains these principles, the voters, putting patriotism ahead of pocketbooks, will give you their applause.

In the future days, which we seek to make secure, we look forward to a world founded upon four essential human freedoms.

The first is freedom of speech and expression—everywhere in the world.

The second is freedom of every person to worship God in his own way—everywhere in the world.

The third is freedom from want—which, translated into world terms, means economic understandings which will secure to every nation a healthy peacetime life for its inhabitants—everywhere in the world.

The fourth is freedom from fear—which, translated into world terms, means a world-wide reduction of armaments to such a point and in such a thorough fashion that no nation will be in a position to commit an act of physical aggression against any neighbor—anywhere in the world.

That is no vision of a distant millennium. It is a definite basis for a kind of world attainable in our own time and generation. That kind of world is the very antithesis of the so-called new order of tyranny which the dictators seek to create with the crash of a bomb.

To that new order we oppose the greater conception—the moral order. A good society is able to face schemes of world domination and foreign revolutions alike without fear.

Since the beginning of our American history, we have been engaged in change—in a perpetual peaceful revolution—a revolution which goes on steadily, quietly adjusting itself to changing conditions—without the concentration camp or the quick-lime in the ditch. The world order which we seek is the cooperation of free countries, working together in a friendly, civilized society.

This nation has placed its destiny in the hands and heads and hearts of its millions of free men and women; and its faith in freedom under the guidance of God. Freedom means the supremacy of human rights everywhere. Our support goes to those who struggle to gain those rights or keep them. Our strength is our unity of purpose. To that high concept there can be no end save victory.

Questions for Discussion

1. According to Roosevelt, why does appeasement no longer work as America's foreign policy?
2. Whom do you think Roosevelt is referring to as "selfish men who would clip the wing of the American eagle to feather their own nests," and what does he mean?
3. How does Roosevelt define a "healthy and strong democracy"? Did these conditions exist in the United States for all Americans in 1941?
4. At the end of the speech, FDR famously identifies "four essential human freedoms." What are these freedoms, and why does he believe they are essential for Americans as well as all people?
5. Should the U.S. government ensure these four freedoms? Why or why not?

Further Reading

Bulosan, Carlos. "Freedom from Want," *Saturday Evening Post*, March 3, 1943.
Executive Order 8802. 1941.
Roosevelt, Franklin Delano. "Quarantine" Speech, Chicago, October 5, 1937.
United Nations. "The Universal Declaration of Human Rights," 1948.

Notes

1. Roosevelt, Address at Oglethorpe University; Roosevelt, Radio Address from Albany, New York, May 22, 1932.
2. Roosevelt, "The 'Forgotten Man' Speech", April 7, 1932.

Notice in San Francisco directing all civilian Japanese and Japanese Americans to depart by April 7, 1942. (posted at First and Front Streets; first area of the city targeted under Executive Order 9066).

16

Executive Order 9066 (1942)

Franklin D. Roosevelt

Introduction

Before the Japanese attack on Pearl Harbor, key decision-makers were already primed to see Japanese American communities as a threat. In 1934, the U.S. State Department issued a dire warning that in the event of war with Japan, West Coast Japanese would betray the United States. That same year, Representative John Dockweiler made the wild assertion that a quarter of Japanese Americans were reserve officers in the Japanese Army. These baseless claims, echoed across government agencies, reveal the entrenched distrust of Japanese immigrants and their American citizen children—a paranoia that would soon justify the wholesale violation of their civil rights.

On December 7, 1941, Japan launched a surprise attack on the Pacific Fleet in Hawaii, followed by strikes on U.S. military bases in the Philippines, Guam, and Wake Island. President Franklin D. Roosevelt, who had been preparing for war, seized the moment to rally a hesitant public. In his "Day of Infamy" speech, he strategically portrayed the assault as an attack on the U.S. mainland, obscuring the territorial status of the places where the attacks occurred. Soon thereafter, *Time* magazine published an article, instructing the American public to identify people of Japanese descent.

Executive Order 9066, issued by President Roosevelt in February 1942, stands as a stark reminder of how wartime hysteria can eclipse the nation's foundational commitment to due process. The order granted military commanders sweeping power to designate "military areas" and expel "any or all persons" from these zones. Though it never explicitly mentioned "Japanese," its intent was unmistakable. Over 112,000 people of Japanese descent—about two-thirds of them U.S. citizens—were forced from their West Coast homes and herded into ten detention camps. Some locations were deliberately chosen to exploit detainees as cheap workers for infrastructure projects, government contractors, and individual farms that had suffered labor shortages during wartime. Though far more numerous, only 2,048 German and 418 Italian citizens were incarcerated as "enemy aliens," showing how the weight of government suspicion does not fall equally on all shoulders. The injustice was not confined to the United States. Peru and other Latin American countries, at the behest of Washington, rounded up 2,300 Japanese Latin Americans and shipped them to Crystal City, Texas.

Japanese Americans resisted the ancestry-based discrimination that propelled wartime incarceration. The U.S. Constitution, particularly the Fifth Amendment, guarantees due process—principles that the enforcement of Executive Order 9066 violated. Fred Korematsu, a twenty-three-year-old U.S. citizen of Japanese descent, was arrested for defying the evacuation order and became the subject of a landmark Supreme Court ruling defending Japanese Americans' constitutional rights. Resistance also emerged from within the camps. At Heart Mountain, draft-aged Japanese American men formed the Fair Play Committee, agitated for the restoration of U.S. citizens' civil rights. They met regularly to share grievances, strategize ways to reclaim their rights, and engage with theories on constitutional law.
—Heather Ruth Lee

>
> Executive Order No. 9066
> The President
> Executive Order
> Authorizing the Secretary of War to Prescribe Military Areas

Whereas the successful prosecution of the war requires every possible protection against espionage and against sabotage to national-defense material, national-defense premises, and national-defense utilities as defined in Section 4, Act of April 20, 1918, 40 Stat. 533, as amended by the Act of November 30, 1940, 54 Stat. 1220, and the Act of August 21, 1941, 55 Stat. 655 (U.S.C., Title 50, Sec. 104);

Now, therefore, by virtue of the authority vested in me as President of the United States, and Commander in Chief of the Army and Navy, I hereby authorize and direct the Secretary of War, and the Military Commanders whom he may from time to time designate, whenever he or any designated Commander deems such action necessary or desirable, to prescribe military areas in such places and of such extent as he or the appropriate Military Commander may determine, from which any or all persons may be excluded, and with respect to which, the right of any person to enter, remain in, or leave shall be subject to whatever restrictions the Secretary of War or the appropriate Military Commander may impose in his discretion. The Secretary of War is hereby authorized to provide for residents of any such area who are excluded therefrom, such transportation, food, shelter, and other accommodations as may be necessary, in the judgment of the Secretary of War or the said Military Commander, and until other arrangements are made, to accomplish the purpose of this order. The designation of military areas in any region or locality shall supersede designations of prohibited and restricted areas by the Attorney General under the Proclamations of December 7 and 8, 1941, and shall supersede the responsibility and authority of the Attorney General under the said Proclamations in respect of such prohibited and restricted areas.

I hereby further authorize and direct the Secretary of War and the said Military Commanders to take such other steps as he or the appropriate Military Commander may deem advisable to enforce compliance with the restrictions applicable to each Military area hereinabove authorized to be designated, including the use of Federal troops and other Federal Agencies, with authority to accept assistance of state and local agencies.

I hereby further authorize and direct all Executive Departments, independent establishments and other Federal Agencies, to assist the Secretary of War or the said Military Commanders in carrying out this Executive Order, including the furnishing of medical aid, hospitalization, food, clothing, transportation, use of land, shelter, and other supplies, equipment, utilities, facilities, and services.

This order shall not be construed as modifying or limiting in any way the authority heretofore granted under Executive Order No. 8972, dated December 12, 1941, nor shall it be construed as limiting or modifying the duty and responsibility of the Federal Bureau of Investigation, with respect to the investigation of alleged acts of sabotage or the duty and responsibility of the Attorney General and the Department of Justice under the Proclamations of December 7 and 8, 1941, prescribing regulations for the conduct and control of alien enemies, except as such duty and responsibility is superseded by the designation of military areas hereunder.

Franklin D. Roosevelt
The White House,
February 19, 1942.

Questions for Discussion

1. In what ways did Executive Order 9066 undermine the legal and social meaning of American citizenship?
2. How does Executive Order 9066 skew the balance of power between the executive branch and constitutional protections, particularly the Fifth Amendment?
3. What does Executive Order 9066 teach about how the federal government can normalize and justify discrimination through bureaucratic structures in times of crisis?
4. What constitutional or legal mechanisms existed to challenge executive overreach and protect civil rights during wartime? Were they sufficient?
5. What can justice and reparations look like for a government-imposed injustice like Executive Order 9066?

Further Reading

Federal Bureau of Investigation. Heart Mountain Fair Play Committee Report. 1944.
"How to Tell your Friends from the Japs," *Time Magazine*, December 22, 1942.
Motion to Vacate Conviction and Dismiss Indictment of Fred T. Korematsu, November 16, 1983. https://www.archives.gov/san-francisco/highlights/Korematsu
Roosevelt, Franklin D. "Day of Infamy." 1941. https://www.archives.gov/publications/prologue/2001/winter/crafting-day-of-infamy-speech.html
U.S. Constitution, amend 5.

DAVID C. MARCUS.
Attorney at Law.
213 Spring & Second Bldg.
Los Angeles, California.
VA. 6311

FILED
MAR 2 - 1945
EDMUND L. SMITH, Clerk
By [signature]
Deputy Clerk

IN THE DISTRICT COURT OF THE UNITED STATES
FOR THE SOUTHERN DISTRICT OF CALIFORNIA
CENTRAL DIVISION

GONZALO MENDEZ and SYLVIA, GONZALO and
GERONIMO MENDEZ, by their father and next
of friend GONZALO MENDEZ,
WILLIAM GUZMAN and BILLY GUZMAN, by his
father and next of friend WILLIAM GUZMAN,
FRANK PALOMINO, and ARTHUR and SALLY
PALOMINO, by their father and next of friend
FRANK PALOMINO,
THOMAS ESTRADA and CLARA, ROBERTO, FRANCISCO,
SYRIA, DANIEL and EVELINA ESTRADA, by their
father and next of friend, THOMAS ESTRADA,
LORENZO RAMIREZ and IGNACIO, SILVERIO and
JOSE RAMIREZ, by their father and next of
friend LORENZO RAMIREZ,

      Petitioners.

      -vs-

WESTMINISTER SCHOOL DISTRICT OF ORANGE COUNTY,
and J. A. HOULIHAN, LEWIS CONRADY, RAY SCHMITT,
as Trustees and J. HARRIS, Superintendent of
said School District,
GARDEN GROVE ELEMENTARY SCHOOL DISTRICT OF
ORANGE COUNTY and WILLIAM C. NOBLE, ROBERT B.
SMITH and PAUL APPLEBURY as Trustees and
JAMES L. KENT, Superintendent of said School
District,
SANTA ANA CITY SCHOOLS and GEORGE R. WELLS,
HIRAM M. CURREY, JAMES K. GIVENS, DANIEL W.
STOVER and GEORGE J. BUSDIEKER its Board of
Education and FRANK A. HENDERSON and HAROLD
YOST, its Superintendent and Secretary,
EL MODENO SCHOOL DISTRICT and HENRY CAMPBELL,
THEODORE HOWER, CLARENCE JOHNSON as Trustees,
and HAROLD HAMMARSTEN, Superintendent of
said School District,

      Respondents.

PETITION

No. 4292-M

March 2, 1945, lawsuit filed by Gonzalo Mendez and five other families against four local school districts in Orange County, California.

17

Mendez v. Westminster (1946)

Paul J. McCormick

Introduction

For Latinos in the Southwest, racial violence and discrimination were commonplace well into the mid-twentieth century. Latinos experienced voter suppression, exclusions from juries, and discriminatory hiring and wage practices. Segregation in theaters, pools, restaurants, and schools was standard throughout the Southwest. An extension of Jim Crow in the South, these practices are referred to by historians as "Juan Crow."

Segregated schools for Mexican Americans remained a usual practice well into the 1940s. At times, Mexican American children attended the same school as their Anglo peers but were taught in separate spaces referred to as "Mexican rooms." The curriculum at these segregated schools focused on work training, industrial skills for the boys, and domestic skills for the girls. The schooling was separate but certainly not equal. Especially after World War II, many Mexican Americans turned to the courts to fight discrimination.

In 1944, Gonzolo (who was Mexican) and Felicitas (who was Puerto Rican) Mendez leased a farm in Westminster, California, from the Munemitsus, a Japanese family who were incarcerated at an internment camp in Arizona. Moving their family to Westminster, the Mendez family became one of the few Latino farmers in the area. When trying to enroll their children Sylvia, Gonzalo Jr., and Jerome in the neighborhood school, the Mendezes were denied and told to enroll at the school reserved for Mexican Americans.

When appealing to local officials proved unsuccessful, Gonzalo Mendez hired a civil rights lawyer, David Marcus. Marcus and Mendez recruited four additional families, one from each of the four school districts in the county, to serve as additional plaintiffs in a class action lawsuit against the Westminster, Garden Grove, El Modena, and Santa Ana boards of education.

The five families filed the class action lawsuit in March 1945. Since Mexicans were considered legally white, the legal team for Mendez did not frame their argument around racial discrimination. Instead, they argued that segregation based on ancestry violated students' Fourteenth Amendment right to equal protection by the state.

On February 18, 1946, U.S. District Court Judge Paul J. McCormick ruled in favor of the plaintiff, Mendez et al., and ordered that the school districts cease segregation. While the Westminster school district agreed with the decision, the three other boards filed appeals, bringing national attention to the case. Thurgood Marshall, on behalf of the NAACP, authored a brief to support the *Mendez* case.

On April 14, 1947, the Ninth Circuit Court of Appeals in San Francisco upheld McCormick's 1946 judgment that one cannot segregate based on national origin or Mexican descent. As a result, California Governor Earl Warren signed a bill that banned school segregation in public schools, making California the first state to outlaw segregation in public schools.

Mendez v. Westminster was an early blow to school segregation as it challenged the "separate but equal" doctrine and paved the way for the desegregation of schools for Latinos in Texas and Arizona. It was also instructive for Thurgood Marshall, who would employ several of the arguments he used in the appeal for this case in the landmark *Brown v. Board of Education* case.—Raquel Escobar

64 F. Supp. 544 (1946)
Mendez et al. v. Westminister School District of Orange County et al.
Civil Action No. 4292.
District Court, S. D. California, Central Division.

Gonzalo Mendez, William Guzman, Frank Palomino, Thomas Estrada and Lorenzo Ramirez, as citizens of the United States, and on behalf of their minor children, and as they allege in the petition, on behalf of "some 5000" persons similarly affected, all of Mexican or Latin descent, have filed a class suit . . .

The complaint, grounded upon the Fourteenth Amendment to the Constitution of the United States and Subdivision 14 of Section 24 of the Judicial Code, Title 28, Section 41, subdivision 14, U.S.C.A., alleges a concerted policy and design of class discrimination against "persons of Mexican or Latin descent or extraction" of elementary school age by the defendant school agencies in the conduct and operation of public schools of said districts, resulting in the denial of the equal protection of the laws to such class of persons among which are the petitioning school children.

Specifically, plaintiffs allege:

"That for several years last past respondents have and do now in furtherance and in execution of their common plan, design and purpose within their respective Systems and Districts, have by their regulation, custom and usage and in execution thereof adopted and declared: That all children or persons of Mexican or Latin descent or extraction, though Citizens of the United States of America, shall be, have been and are now excluded from attending, using, enjoying and receiving the benefits of the education, health and recreation facilities of certain schools within their respective Districts and Systems but that said children are now and have been segregated and required to and must attend and use certain schools in said Districts and Systems reserved for and attended solely and exclusively by children and persons of Mexican and Latin descent, while such other schools are maintained, attended and used exclusively by and for persons and children purportedly known as White or Anglo-Saxon children.

"That in execution of said rules and regulations, each, every and all the foregoing children are compelled and required to and must attend and use the schools in said respective Districts reserved for and attended solely and exclusively by children of Mexican and Latin descent and are forbidden, barred and excluded from attending any other school in said District or System solely for the reason that said children or child are of Mexican or Latin descent."

The petitioners demand that the alleged rules, regulations, customs and usages be adjudged void and unconstitutional and that an injunction issue restraining further application by defendant school authorities of such rules, regulations, customs, and usages.

It is conceded by all parties that there is no question of race discrimination in this action. It is, however, admitted that segregation per se is practiced in the above-mentioned school districts as the Spanish-speaking children enter school life and as they advance through the grades in the respective school districts. It is also admitted by the defendants that the petitioning children are qualified to attend the public schools in the respective districts of their residences.

In the Westminster, Garden Grove and El Modeno school districts the respective boards of trustees had taken official action, declaring that there be no segregation of pupils on a racial basis but that non-English-speaking children (which group, excepting as to a small number of pupils, was made up entirely of children of Mexican ancestry or descent), be required to attend schools designated by the boards separate and apart from English-speaking pupils; that such group should attend such schools until they had acquired some proficiency in the English language.

The petitioners contend that such official action evinces a covert attempt by the school authorities in such school districts to produce an arbitrary discrimination against school children of Mexican extraction or descent and that such illegal result has been established in such school districts respectively. The school authorities of the City of Santa Ana have not memorialized any such official action, but petitioners assert that the same custom and usage exists in the schools of the City of Santa Ana under the authority of appropriate school agencies of such city.

The concrete acts complained of are those of the various school district officials in directing which schools the petitioning children and others of the same class or group must attend. The segregation exists in the elementary schools to and including the sixth grade in two of the defendant districts, and in the two other defendant districts through the eighth grade. The record before us shows without conflict that the technical facilities and physical conveniences offered in the schools housing entirely the segregated pupils, the efficiency of the teachers therein and the curricula are identical and in some respects superior to those in the other schools in the respective districts.

The ultimate question for decision may be thus stated: Does such official action of defendant district school agencies and the usages and practices pursued by the respective school authorities as shown by the evidence operate to deny or deprive the so-called non-English-speaking school children of Mexican ancestry or descent within such school districts of the equal protection of the laws? . . .

We therefore turn to consider whether under the record before us the school boards and administrative authorities in the respective defendant districts have by their segregation policies and practices transgressed applicable law and Constitutional safeguards and limitations and thus have invaded the personal right which every public school pupil has to the equal protection provision of the Fourteenth Amendment to obtain the means of education.

We think the pattern of public education promulgated in the Constitution of California and effectuated by provisions of the Education Code of the State prohibits segregation of the pupils of Mexican ancestry in the elementary schools from the rest of the school children.

. . . The common segregation attitudes and practices of the school authorities in the defendant school districts in Orange County pertain solely to children of Mexican ancestry and parentage. They are singled out as a class for segregation. . . .

Obviously, the children referred to in these laws are those of Mexican ancestry. And it is noteworthy that the educational advantages of their commingling with other pupils is regarded as being so important to the school system of the State that it is provided for even regardless of the citizenship of the parents. We perceive in the laws relating to the public educational system in the State of California a clear purpose to avoid and forbid distinctions among pupils based upon race or ancestry except in specific situations not pertinent to this action. Distinctions of that kind have recently been declared by the highest judicial authority of the United States "by their very nature odious to a free people whose institutions are founded upon the doctrine of equality." They are said to be "utterly inconsistent with American traditions and ideals." *Kiyoshi Hirabayashi v. United States*, 320 U.S. 81 . . .

Our conclusions in this action, however, do not rest solely upon what we conceive to be the utter irreconcilability of the segregation practices in the defendant school districts with the public educational system authorized and sanctioned by the laws of the State of California. We think such practices clearly and unmistakably disregard rights secured by the supreme law of the land. *Cumming v. Board of Education of Richmond County*, supra.

"The equal protection of the laws" pertaining to the public school system in California is not provided by furnishing in separate schools the same technical facilities, text books and courses of instruction to children of Mexican ancestry that are available to the other public school children regardless of their ancestry. A paramount requisite in the American system of public education is social equality. It must be open to all children by unified school association regardless of lineage.

We think that under the record before us the only tenable ground upon which segregation practices in the defendant school districts can be defended lies in the English language deficiencies of some of the children of Mexican ancestry as they enter elementary public school life as beginners. But even such situations do not justify the general and continuous segregation in separate schools of the children of Mexican ancestry from the rest of the elementary school population as has been shown to be the practice in the defendant school districts in all of them to the sixth grade, and in two of them through the eighth grade.

The evidence clearly shows that Spanish-speaking children are retarded in learning English by lack of exposure to its use because of segregation, and that commingling of the entire student body instills and develops a common cultural attitude among the school children which is imperative for the perpetuation of American institutions and ideals. It is also established by the record that the methods of segregation prevalent in the defendant school districts foster antagonisms in the children and suggest inferiority among them where none exists....

In Garden Grove Elementary School District the segregation extends only through the fifth grade. Beyond, all pupils in such district, regardless of their ancestry or linguistic proficiency, are housed, instructed and associate in the same school facility.

This arrangement conclusively refutes the reasonableness or advisability of any segregation of children of Mexican ancestry beyond the fifth grade in any of the defendant school districts in view of the standardized and uniform curricular requirements in the elementary schools of Orange County.

But the admitted practice and long established custom in this school district whereby all elementary public school children of Mexican descent are required to attend one specified school (the Hoover) until they attain the sixth grade, while all other pupils of the same grade are permitted to and do attend two other elementary schools of this district, notwithstanding that some of such pupils live within the Hoover School division of the district, clearly establishes an unfair and arbitrary class distinction in the system of public education operative in the Garden Grove Elementary School District.

The long-standing discriminatory custom prevalent in this district is aggravated by the fact shown by the record that although there are approximately 25 children of Mexican descent living in the vicinity of the Lincoln School, none of them attend that school, but all are peremptorily assigned by the school authorities to the Hoover School, although the evidence shows that there are no school zones territorially established in the district.

... Segregation of these from the rest of the school population precipitated such vigorous protests by residents of the district that the school board in January, 1944, recognizing the discriminatory results of segregation, resolved to unite the two schools and thus abolish the objectionable practices which had been operative in the schools of the district for a considerable period. A bond issue was submitted to the electors to raise funds to defray the cost of contemplated expenditures in the school consolidation. The bonds were not voted and the record before us in this action reflects no execution or carrying out of the official action of the board of trustees ... It thus appears that there has been no abolishment of the traditional segregation practices in this district pertaining to pupils of Mexican ancestry through the gamut of elementary school life....

Before considering the specific factual situation in the Santa Ana City Schools it should be noted that the omnibus segregation of children of Mexican ancestry from the rest of the student body in the elementary grades in the schools involved in this case because of language handicaps is not warranted by the record before us. The tests applied to the beginners are shown to have been generally hasty, superficial and not reliable. In some instances separate classification was determined largely by the Latinized or Mexican name of the child. Such methods of evaluating language knowledge are illusory and are not conducive to the inculcation and enjoyment of civil rights which are of primary importance in the public school system of education in the United States.

It has been held that public school authorities may differentiate in the exercise of their reasonable discretion as to the pedagogical methods of instruction to be pursued with different pupils. And foreign language handicaps may be to such a degree in the pupils in elementary schools as to require special treatment in separate classrooms. Such separate allocations, however, can be lawfully made only after credible examination by the appropriate school authority of each child whose capacity to learn is under consideration and the determination of such segregation must be based wholly upon indiscriminate foreign language impediments in the individual child, regardless of his ethnic traits or ancestry....

The natural operation and effect of the Board's official action manifests a clear purpose to arbitrarily discriminate against the pupils of Mexican ancestry and to deny to them the equal protection of the laws....

There are other discriminatory customs, shown by the evidence, existing in the defendant school districts as to pupils of Mexican descent and extraction, but we deem it unnecessary to discuss them in this memorandum.

We conclude by holding that the allegations of the complaint (petition) have been established sufficiently to justify injunctive relief against all defendants, restraining further discriminatory practices against the pupils of Mexican descent in the public schools of defendant school districts. . . .

Questions for Discussion

1. What discrimination and unequal treatment does the lawsuit mention?
2. Why does the discussion of language skills play an important role in this case?
3. Closely read the paragraph that begins "Our conclusion in this action," and the next paragraph. In your own words, explain what these paragraphs mean and what they are saying about the practices of these school districts?
4. Why did Mendez and others facing school segregation object to "separate but equal" schools? Why do you think the federal courts did not address the separate but equal doctrine?
5. What does full citizenry mean for Mexican Americans when navigating the system of Jim Crow/Juan Crow?

Further Reading

Alvarez v. Lemon Grove, No. 66625 (San Diego County, 1931). [See also the documentary at https://www.pbs.org/video/the-lemon-grove-incident-gcrfxv/]

Delgado v. Bastrop Independent School District, (1948). https://texashistory.unt.edu/ark:/67531/metapth248859/

Hernandez v. Texas, 347 U.S. 475 (1954). https://www.loc.gov/item/usrep347475/

Katzenbach v. Morgan, 384 U.S. 641 (1966). https://www.loc.gov/item/usrep384641/

Treaty of Guadalupe Hidalgo. 1848. https://www.archives.gov/milestone-documents/treaty-of-guadalupe-hidalgo

Westminster School District of Orange County v. Mendez. Brief amicus curie for the National Association for the Advancement of Colored People. 1945. https://archive.org/details/NAACPWestminsterBrief/page/n5/mode/2up

Notes

1. "Section 1. All persons born or naturalized in the United States, and subject to the jurisdiction thereof, are citizens of the United States and of the State wherein they reside. No State shall make or enforce any law which shall abridge the privileges or immunities of citizens of the United States; nor shall any State deprive

any person of life, liberty, or property, without due process of law; nor deny to any person within its jurisdiction the equal protection of the laws."

2. "The district courts shall have original jurisdiction as follows: * * *"

Sec. 41, subd. (14) "Suits to redress deprivation of civil rights. Fourteenth. Of all suits at law or in equity authorized by law to be brought by any person to redress the deprivation, under color of any law, statute, ordinance, regulation, custom, or usage, of any State, of any right, privilege, or immunity, secured by the Constitution of the United States, or of any right secured by any law of the United States providing for equal rights of citizens of the United States, or of all persons within the jurisdiction of the United States."

3. Sec. 8501, Education Code. "The day elementary school of each school district shall be open for the admission of all children between six and 21 years of age residing within the boundaries of the district." See also Sec. 8002. "The governing board of any school district shall maintain all of the elementary day schools established by it, and all of the day high schools established by it with equal rights and privileges as far as possible."

4. Sec. 8003. "Schools for Indian children, and children of Chinese, Japanese, or Mongolian parentage . . ."

5. The study of American institutions and ideals in all schools located within the State of California is required by Section 10051, Education Code.

THE NATION'S CAPITAL
A SYMBOL OF FREEDOM AND EQUALITY?

IF HE DECIDES TO REMAIN IN D. C. OVERNIGHT HE WILL FIND THAT:

HE CANNOT EAT IN A DOWNTOWN RESTAURANT. HE CANNOT ATTEND A DOWNTOWN MOVIE OR PLAY. HE CANNOT SLEEP IN A DOWNTOWN HOTEL.

IF HE DECIDES TO STAY IN D. C.

➤ HE USUALLY MUST FIND A HOME IN AN OVERCROWDED, SUB-STANDARD, SEGREGATED AREA:

NEGRO-OCCUPIED DWELLINGS
40% SUBSTANDARD

WHITE-OCCUPIED DWELLINGS
12% SUBSTANDARD

➤ HE MUST SEND HIS CHILDREN TO INFERIOR JIM CROW SCHOOLS: ➤ HE MUST ENTRUST HIS FAMILY'S HEALTH TO MEDICAL AGENCIES WHICH GIVE THEM INFERIOR SERVICES:

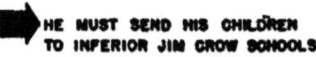

WHITES — CAPACITY EXCEEDS ENROLLMENT BY 27%
NEGROES — ENROLLMENT EXCEEDS CAPACITY BY 8%

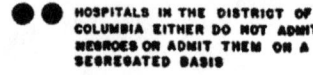
●● HOSPITALS IN THE DISTRICT OF COLUMBIA EITHER DO NOT ADMIT NEGROES OR ADMIT THEM ON A SEGREGATED BASIS

88

Several diagrams accompanied the text of the Truman Commission report, including this one in the section on "Civil Rights in the Nation's Capital." To Secure These Rights, the Report of the President's Committee on Civil Rights, Washington: U.S. Govt. (Print. 1947)

18

To Secure These Rights (1947)
The President's Committee on Civil Rights

Introduction

After the United States defeated the fascist Axis powers in the Second World War, Americans sought to understand the meaning of this victory for their own democracy. Many Black soldiers, symbolized by the *Pittsburgh Courier*'s Double V campaign, sought their own victory for civil rights at home after having helped defend democracy abroad. Emboldened by the 1944 Supreme Court decision, *Smith v. Allwright,* which outlawed all-white political primaries, African Americans and their allies attempted to foment a postwar democratic freedom struggle. But southern Democrats, allied with other conservative politicians and interest groups, intended to preserve Jim Crow apartheid in the South and push back against enforcing citizenship rights nationwide.

President Harry Truman, Roosevelt's successor, felt pressure from all sides to articulate a vision for American democracy in the postwar. Truman had no previous record of civil rights advocacy at home in Missouri, but he did seem genuinely appalled by incidents of postwar white supremacy. When in February 1946 police in South Carolina beat Black veteran Isaac Woodard so badly they permanently blinded him, Truman ordered a federal investigation and created the President's Committee on Civil Rights.

But Truman's moral repugnance was not his only motivation; he also saw civil rights in relation to the dawn of the Cold War. In March 1947, Truman gave a speech outlining a new foreign policy against Communism. "At the present moment in world history," he said, "nearly every nation must choose between alternative ways of life." The first way consisted of "free institutions, representative government, free elections, guarantees of individual liberty, freedom of speech and religion, and freedom from political oppression" while the second relied "upon terror and oppression, a controlled press and radio; fixed elections, and the suppression of personal freedoms."* This speech not only signaled a new foreign policy but also a new domestic policy that would use anti-Communism as a weapon to delegitimize anyone in America who pushed for systemic reform. The federal government subsequently fired, blacklisted, jailed, deported, and marginalized many civil rights, labor, and other activists. Yet, this new Cold War politics also opened new leverage in support of civil rights. Proponents of civil rights began to shame the United States for permitting racial discrimination while extolling its democracy to the rest of the world. They effectively argued that the Cold War effort to gain allies could become compromised by U.S. hypocrisy in a world primarily made up of people of color.

Truman barely won the presidential election in 1948 over Republican Thomas Dewey. The Democratic Party seemed to be coming apart over the issue of civil rights and, aside from one speech in Harlem, Truman downplayed civil rights on the campaign trail. Yet, just months before the election, eyeing the possible swing votes of African Americans and liberals in the North, Truman issued Executive Order 9981, which mandated an end to racial segregation in the military. During Truman's second term, southern Senators filibustered any proposed civil rights legislation, thus thwarting the prescriptions by the Committee on Civil Rights. But the underlying urgency to redress anti-democratic discrimination remained, and "To Secure These Rights" would become a remarkable liberal blueprint for civil rights legislation and enforcement in subsequent decades.—Erik S. Gellman

Chapter IV

A Program of Action: The Committee's Recommendations

THE TIME IS NOW

TWICE BEFORE in American history the nation has found it necessary to review the state of its civil rights. The first time was during the 15 years between 1776 and 1791, from the drafting of the Declaration of Independence through the Articles of Confederation experiment to the writing of the Constitution and the Bill of Rights. It was then that

---

*Harry S. Truman, Address Before a Joint Session of Congress, March 12, 1947, Avalon Project: Documents in Law, History and Diplomacy, Lillian Goldman Law Library, Yale Law School.

the distinctively American heritage was finally distilled from earlier views of liberty. The second time was when the Union was temporarily sundered over the question of whether it could exist "half-slave" and "half-free."

It is our profound conviction that we have come to a time for a third re-examination of the situation, and a sustained drive ahead. Our reasons for believing this are those of conscience, of self-interest, and of survival in a threatening world. Or to put it another way, we have a moral reason, an economic reason, and an international reason for believing that the time for action is now.

The Moral Reason

We have considered the American heritage of freedom at some length. We need no further justification for a broad and immediate program than the need to reaffirm our faith in the traditional American morality. The pervasive gap between our aims and what we actually do is creating a kind of moral dry rot which eats away at the emotional and rational bases of democratic beliefs. There are times when the difference between what we preach about civil rights and what we practice is shockingly illustrated by individual outrages. There are times when the whole structure of our ideology is made ridiculous by individual instances. And there are certain continuing, quiet, omnipresent practices which do irreparable damage to our beliefs.

As examples of "moral erosion" there are the consequences of suffrage limitations in the South. The fact that Negroes and many whites have not been allowed to vote in some states has actually sapped the morality underlying universal suffrage. Many men in public and private life do not believe that those who have been kept from voting are capable of self rule. They finally convince themselves that disfranchised people do not really have the right to vote.

Wartime segregation in the armed forces is another instance of how a social pattern may wreak moral havoc. Practically all white officers and enlisted men in all branches of service saw Negro military personnel performing only the most menial functions. They saw Negroes recruited for the common defense treated as men apart and distinct from themselves. As a result, men who might otherwise have maintained the equalitarian morality of their forebears were given reason to look down on their fellow citizens. This has been sharply illustrated by the Army study discussed previously, in which white servicemen expressed great surprise at the excellent performance of Negroes who joined them in the firing line. Even now, very few people know of the successful experiment with integrated combat units. Yet it is important in explaining why some Negro troops did not do well; it is proof that equal treatment can produce equal performance.

Thousands upon thousands of small, unseen incidents reinforce the impact of headlined violations like lynchings, and broad social patterns like segregation and inequality of treatment. . . .

It is impossible to decide who suffers the greatest moral damage from our civil rights transgressions, because all of us are hurt. That is certainly true of those who are victimized. Their belief in the basic truth of the American promise is undermined. But they do have the realization, galling as it sometimes is, of being morally in the right. The damage to those who are responsible for these violations of our moral standards may well be greater. They, too, have been reared to honor the command of "free and equal." And all of us must share in the shame at the growth of hypocrisies . . . All of us must endure the cynicism about democratic values which our failures breed.

The United States can no longer countenance these burdens on its common conscience, these inroads on its moral fiber.

The Economic Reason

One of the principal economic problems facing us and the rest of the world is achieving maximum production and continued prosperity. The loss of a huge, potential market for goods is a direct result of the economic discrimination which is practiced against many of our minority groups. A sort of vicious circle is produced. Discrimination depresses the wages and income of minority groups. As a result, their purchasing power is curtailed and markets are reduced. Reduced markets result in reduced production. This cuts down employment, which of course means lower wages and still fewer job opportunities. Rising fear, prejudice, and insecurity aggravate the very discrimination in employment which sets the vicious circle in motion. . . .

Economic discrimination prevents full use of all our resources. During the war, when we were called upon to make an all-out productive effort, we found that we lacked skilled laborers. This shortage might not have been so serious if minorities had not frequently been denied opportunities for training and experience. In the end, it cost large amounts of money and precious time to provide ourselves with trained persons.

Discrimination imposes a direct cost upon our economy through the wasteful duplication of many facilities and services required by the "separate but equal" policy. That the resources of the South are sorely strained by the burden of a double system of schools and other public services has already been indicated. Segregation is also economically wasteful for private business. Public transportation companies must often provide duplicate facilities to serve majority and minority groups separately. Places of public accommodation and recreation reject business when it comes in the form of unwanted persons. Stores reduce their sales by turning away minority customers. Factories must provide separate locker rooms, pay windows, drinking fountains, and wash-rooms for the different groups.

Discrimination in wage scales and hiring policies forces a higher proportion of some minority groups onto relief rolls than corresponding segments of the majority. A study by the Federal Emergency Relief Administration during the depression of the Thirties revealed that in every region the percentage of Negro families on relief was far greater than white families.

Similarly, the rates of disease, crime, and fires are disproportionately great in areas which are economically depressed as compared with wealthier areas. Many of the prominent American minorities are confined by economic discrimination, by law, by restrictive covenants, and by social pressure to the most dilapidated, undesirable locations. Property in these locations yields a smaller return in taxes, which is seldom sufficient to meet the inordinately high cost of public services in depressed areas. The majority pays a high price in taxes for the low status of minorities.

To the costs of discrimination must be added the expensive investigations, trials, and property losses which result from civil rights violations. In the aggregate, these attain huge proportions. The 1943 Detroit riot alone resulted in the destruction of two million dollars in property.

Finally, the cost of prejudice cannot be computed in terms of markets, production, and expenditures. Perhaps the most expensive results are the least tangible ones. No nation can afford to have its component groups hostile toward one another without feeling the stress. People who live in a state of tension and suspicion cannot use their energy constructively. The frustrations of their restricted existence are translated into aggression against the dominant group....

The United States can no longer afford this heavy drain upon its human wealth, its national competence.

The International Reason

Our position in the postwar world is so vital to the future that our smallest actions have far-reaching effects. We have come to know that our own security in a highly interdependent world is inextricably tied to the security and well-being of all people and all countries. Our foreign policy is designed to make the United States an enormous, positive influence for peace and progress throughout the world. We have tried to let nothing, not even extreme political differences between ourselves and foreign nations, stand in the way of this goal. But our domestic civil rights shortcomings are a serious obstacle....

The people of the United States stem from many lands. Other nations and their citizens are naturally intrigued by what has happened to their American "relatives." Discrimination against, or mistreatment of, any racial, religious or national group in the United States is not only seen as our internal problem. The dignity of a country, a continent, or even a major portion of the world's population, may be outraged by it. A relatively few individuals here may be identified with millions of people elsewhere, and the way in which they are treated may have world-wide repercussions. We have fewer than half a million American Indians; there are 30 million more in the Western Hemisphere. Our Mexican American and Hispano groups are not large; millions in Central and South America consider them kin. We number our citizens of Oriental descent in the hundreds of thousands; their counterparts overseas are numbered in hundreds of millions. Throughout the Pacific, Latin America, Africa, the Near, Middle, and Far East, the treatment which our Negroes receive is taken as a reflection of our attitudes toward all dark-skinned peoples.

In the recent war, citizens of a dozen European nations were happy to meet Smiths, Cartiers, O'Haras, Schultzes, di Salvos, Cohens, and Sklodowskas and all the others in our armies. Each nation could share in our victories because its "sons" had helped win them. How much of this good feeling was dissipated when they found virulent prejudice among some of our troops is impossible to say.

We cannot escape the fact that our civil rights record has been an issue in world politics. The world's press and radio are full of it. This Committee has seen a multitude of samples. We and our friends have been, and are, stressing our achievements. Those with competing philosophies have stressed—and are shamelessly distorting—our shortcomings. They have not only tried to create hostility toward us among specific nations, races, and religious groups. They have tried to prove our democracy an empty fraud, and our nation a consistent oppressor of underprivileged people. This may seem ludicrous to Americans, but it is sufficiently important to worry our friends. The following United Press dispatch from London proves that (*Washington Post*, May 25, 1947):

> Although the Foreign Office reserved comment on recent lynch activities in the Carolinas, British diplomatic circles said privately today that they have played into the hands of Communist propagandists in Europe * * *.
>
> Diplomatic circles said the two incidents of mob violence would provide excellent propaganda ammunition for Communist agents who have been decrying America's brand of "freedom" and "democracy."
>
> News of the North Carolina kidnaping was prominently displayed by London papers * * *.

The international reason for acting to secure our civil rights now is not to win the approval of our totalitarian critics. We would not expect it if our record were spotless; to them our civil rights record is only a convenient weapon with which to attack us. Certainly we would like to deprive them of that weapon. But we are more concerned with the good opinion of the peoples of the world. Our achievements in building and maintaining a state dedicated to the fundamentals of freedom have already served as a guide for those seeking the best road from chaos to liberty and prosperity. But it is not indelibly written that democracy will encompass the world. We are convinced that our way of life—the free way of life—holds a promise of hope for all people. We have what is perhaps the greatest responsibility ever placed upon a people to keep this promise alive. Only still greater achievements will do it.

The United States is not so strong, the final triumph of the democratic ideal is not so inevitable that we can ignore what the world thinks of us or our record.

Questions for Discussion

1. Why does the committee state that the need for evaluating the nation's civil rights has arisen a third time in 1947? (Compare this moment to the report's mention of the earlier two times as well as the previous documents in this reader).
2. What does the committee mean in arguing that a "moral dry rot" has increasingly compromised the foundations of American democracy?
3. How does the Committee argue that the economy would benefit if the government endorsed and enforced civil rights laws?
4. Why does the Committee invoke an urgent need to prove the United States's democratic intent to the rest of the world?
5. Once you have read the documents *Brown v. Board of Education*, "Letter from Birmingham Jail," and the Equal Rights Amendment, consider how this 1947 report reflects or diverges from those documents' justifications for ensuring democracy for all citizens.
6. Look up the biography of one of the authors of "To Secure These Rights." How does that author's biography help explain why he or she was selected to serve on the President's committee, and how do you think that author shaped the content of the report?

Further Reading

Ephron, Jamila, dir. *The Blinding of Isaac Woodard*. 2021. American Experience.
Executive Order 9981. 1948.
The President's Committee on Civil Rights. "To Secure These Rights: The Report of the President's Committee on Civil Rights." 1947.
Smith v. Allwright, 321 U.S. 649 (1944).
Truman, Harry. "Address in Harlem," Speech, New York, October 29, 1948.
Truman, Harry. "Truman Doctrine." Speech, Washington, DC. March 12, 1947.

Earl Warren as governor of California in about 1950. (Library of Congress, Prints and Photographs division.)

19

Brown v. Board of Education of Topeka (1954)
Earl Warren

Introduction

Initially introduced in 1892 through the United States Supreme Court case *Plessy v. Ferguson*, the question of separate but equal accommodations would persist in the twentieth century. The National Association for the Advancement of Colored People (NAACP) challenged it in the realm of education and pushed for "complete equality in facilities governed by the separate-but-equal rule." This strategic focus can be seen in *Sweatt v. Painter* (1950) and *McLaurin v. Oklahoma State Regents* (1950), both of which were unanimously decided in favor of the Black plaintiffs. In the former, the NAACP argued that Texas's segregated Black law school was unfairly insufficient in both quality of material conditions and "those qualities which are incapable of objective measurement but which make for greatness in a law school."[1] In the latter, the court decided that segregating a student within a university would "impair and inhibit his ability to study, to engage in discussions and exchange views with other students, and in general, to learn his profession."[2]

The NAACP increasingly began "charging segregated education with being discriminatory per se, even if the facilities were equal." Widening its scope, the organization turned to elementary and high schools, which were compulsory, unlike the graduate and professional schools in *Sweatt* or *McLaurin*. They took up Oliver Brown's case for his daughter Linda to attend an all-white school a few blocks from their home rather than a Black school which was further away.[3] Though decided in the plaintiffs' favor, the *Brown* decision was "neither universally accepted nor consistently enforced" and challenges persisted for decades. In North Carolina's Triangle region, "desegregation was achieved in many places, but widespread integration happened almost nowhere." In *Brown*'s aftermath, "most southern black children continued to suffer the psychological consequences of segregation, while a minority assumed the often considerable psychological and physical risks of attending newly integrated public schools." These were a long overdue enforcement effort over the Fourteenth Amendment's equal protection clause.[4]

The following text is the unanimous decision that Chief Justice Earl Warren delivered on May 17, 1954.—Antwain K. Hunter

Opinion
Mr. Chief Justice Warren delivered the opinion of the Court.

These cases come to us from the States of Kansas, South Carolina, Virginia, and Delaware. They are premised on different facts and different local conditions, but a common legal question justifies their consideration together in this consolidated opinion.

In each of the cases, minors of the Negro race, through their legal representatives, seek the aid of the courts in obtaining admission to the public schools of their community on a nonsegregated basis. In each instance, they had been denied admission to schools attended by white children under laws requiring or permitting segregation according to race. This segregation was alleged to deprive the plaintiffs of the equal protection of the laws under the Fourteenth Amendment . . .

The plaintiffs contend that segregated public schools are not "equal" and cannot be made "equal," and that hence they are deprived of the equal protection of the laws. Because of the obvious importance of the question presented, the Court took jurisdiction. Argument was heard in the 1952 Term, and reargument was heard this Term on certain questions propounded by the Court.

Reargument was largely devoted to the circumstances surrounding the adoption of the Fourteenth Amendment in 1868. It covered exhaustively consideration of the Amendment in Congress, ratification by the states, then-existing practices in racial segregation, and the views of proponents and opponents of the Amendment. This discussion and our own investigation convince us that, although these sources cast some light, it is not enough to resolve the problem with which we are faced. At best, they are inconclusive. The most avid proponents of the post-War Amendments undoubtedly intended them to remove all legal distinctions among "all persons born or naturalized in the United States." Their opponents, just as certainly, were antagonistic to both the letter and the spirit of the Amendments and wished them to have the most limited effect. What others in

Congress and the state legislatures had in mind cannot be determined with any degree of certainty.

An additional reason for the inconclusive nature of the Amendment's history with respect to segregated schools is the status of public education at that time. In the South, the movement toward free common schools, supported by general taxation, had not yet taken hold. Education of white children was largely in the hands of private groups. Education of Negroes was almost nonexistent, and practically all of the race were illiterate. In fact, any education of Negroes was forbidden by law in some states. Today, in contrast, many Negroes have achieved outstanding success in the arts and sciences, as well as in the business and professional world. It is true that public school education at the time of the Amendment had advanced further in the North, but the effect of the Amendment on Northern States was generally ignored in the congressional debates. Even in the North, the conditions of public education did not approximate those existing today. The curriculum was usually rudimentary; ungraded schools were common in rural areas; the school term was but three months a year in many states, and compulsory school attendance was virtually unknown. As a consequence, it is not surprising that there should be so little in the history of the Fourteenth Amendment relating to its intended effect on public education.

In the first cases in this Court construing the Fourteenth Amendment, decided shortly after its adoption, the Court interpreted it as proscribing all state-imposed discriminations against the Negro race. The doctrine of "separate but equal" did not make its appearance in this Court until 1896 in the case of *Plessy* v. *Ferguson*, supra, involving not education but transportation. American courts have since labored with the doctrine for over half a century. In this Court, there have been six cases involving the "separate but equal" doctrine in the field of public education. In *Cumming* v. *County Board of Education*, 175 U.S. 528, and *Gong Lum* v. *Rice*, 275 U.S. 78, the validity of the doctrine itself was not challenged. In more recent cases, all on the graduate school level, inequality was found in that specific benefits enjoyed by white students were denied to Negro students of the same educational qualifications. *Missouri ex rel. Gaines* v. *Canada*, 305 U.S. 337; *Sipuel* v. *Oklahoma*, 332 U.S. 631; *Sweatt* v. *Painter*, 339 U.S. 629; *McLaurin* v. *Oklahoma State Regents*, 339 U.S. 637. In none of these cases was it necessary to reexamine the doctrine to grant relief to the Negro plaintiff. And in *Sweatt* v. *Painter*, supra, the Court expressly reserved decision on the question whether *Plessy* v. *Ferguson* should be held inapplicable to public education.

In the instant cases, that question is directly presented. Here, unlike *Sweatt v. Painter*, there are findings below that the Negro and white schools involved have been equalized, or are being equalized, with respect to buildings, curricula, qualifications and salaries of teachers, and other "tangible" factors. Our decision, therefore, cannot turn on merely a comparison of these tangible factors in the Negro and white schools involved in each of the cases. We must look instead to the effect of segregation itself on public education.

In approaching this problem, we cannot turn the clock back to 1868, when the Amendment was adopted, or even to 1896, when *Plessy v. Ferguson* was written. We must consider public education in the light of its full development and its present place in American life throughout the Nation. Only in this way can it be determined if segregation in public schools deprives these plaintiffs of the equal protection of the laws.

Today, education is perhaps the most important function of state and local governments. Compulsory school attendance laws and the great expenditures for education both demonstrate our recognition of the importance of education to our democratic society. It is required in the performance of our most basic public responsibilities, even service in the armed forces. It is the very foundation of good citizenship. Today it is a principal instrument in awakening the child to cultural values, in preparing him for later professional training, and in helping him to adjust normally to his environment. In these days, it is doubtful that any child may reasonably be expected to succeed in life if he is denied the opportunity of an education. Such an opportunity, where the state has undertaken to provide it, is a right which must be made available to all on equal terms.

We come then to the question presented: Does segregation of children in public schools solely on the basis of race, even though the physical facilities and other "tangible" factors may be equal, deprive the children of the minority group of equal educational opportunities? We believe that it does.

In *Sweatt v. Painter*, supra, in finding that a segregated law school for Negroes could not provide them equal educational opportunities, this Court relied in large part on "those qualities which are incapable of objective measurement but which make for greatness in a law school." In *McLaurin v. Oklahoma State Regents*, supra, the Court, in requiring that a Negro admitted to a white graduate school be treated like all other students, again resorted to intangible considerations: ". . . his ability to study, to engage in discussions and exchange views with other students, and, in general, to learn his profession." Such considerations apply with added force to children in grade and high schools. To separate them from others of similar age and qualifications solely because of their race generates a feeling of inferiority as to their status in the community that may affect their hearts and minds in a way unlikely ever to be undone. The effect of this separation on their educational opportunities was well stated by a finding in the Kansas case by a court which nevertheless felt compelled to rule against the Negro plaintiffs:

Segregation of white and colored children in public schools has a detrimental effect upon the colored children. The impact is greater when it has the sanction of the law, for the policy of separating the races is usually interpreted as denoting the inferiority of the negro group. A sense of inferiority affects the motivation of a child to learn. Segregation with the sanction of law, therefore, has a tendency to [retard] the educational and mental development of negro children and to deprive them of some of the benefits they would receive in a racial[ly] integrated school system.

Whatever may have been the extent of psychological knowledge at the time of *Plessy* v. *Ferguson*, this finding is amply supported by modern authority. Any language in *Plessy* v. *Ferguson* contrary to this finding is rejected.

We conclude that, in the field of public education, the doctrine of "separate but equal" has no place. Separate educational facilities are inherently unequal. Therefore, we hold that the plaintiffs and others similarly situated for whom the actions have been brought are, by reason of the segregation complained of, deprived of the equal protection of the laws guaranteed by the Fourteenth Amendment. This disposition makes unnecessary any discussion whether such segregation also violates the Due Process Clause of the Fourteenth Amendment.

Because these are class actions, because of the wide applicability of this decision, and because of the great variety of local conditions, the formulation of decrees in these cases presents problems of considerable complexity. On reargument, the consideration of appropriate relief was necessarily subordinated to the primary question—the constitutionality of segregation in public education. We have now announced that such segregation is a denial of the equal protection of the laws . . .

Questions for Discussion

1. How does the *Brown v. Board* decision connect to the Fourteenth Amendment? What does this tell us about the intervening years?

2. Earl Warren declared that "today, education is perhaps the most important function of state and local governments" and also called it "the very foundation of good citizenship." What do you think of these assertions? How does education relate to democracy? What role does the federal government have in education?
3. What do you think of the intangible factors that the court points to in addition to the "buildings, curricula, qualifications and salaries of teachers, and other 'tangible' factors"?
4. Warren references *Plessy v. Ferguson*, which introduced "separate but equal" into the legal landscape. What did the change from *Plessy* to *Brown* mean for American democracy?
5. They are separated by a decade, but how does the *Brown* decision compare and contrast with Martin Luther King Jr.'s "Letter from a Birmingham Jail"?
6. Should public school districts be allowed to specifically tailor their student bodies in order to achieve diversity?

Further Reading

McLaurin v. Oklahoma State Regents, 339 U.S. 637 (1950). [See opinion by Vinson.]
Parents Involved in Community Schools v. Seattle School District No. 1, 551 U.S. 701 (2007). [See opinions by Roberts, Kennedy, and Breyer.]
Plessy v. Ferguson, 163 U.S. 537 (1896). [See opinion by Harlan.]
Sweatt v. Painter, 339 U.S. 629 (1950). [See opinion by Vinson.]
Smith, Howard. "The Southern Manifesto." Speech, Washington, DC. March 12, 1956.
United States Constitution, amend 14, sec 1.

Notes

1. *Plessy v. Ferguson*, 163 U.S. 537 (1896); *Sweatt v. Painter*, 339 U.S. 629 (1950).
2. *McLaurin v. Oklahoma* State Regents, 339 U.S. 637 (1950).
3. Harvard Sitkoff, *The Struggle for Black Equality* (Hill and Wang, 1981), 19–20.
4. Leanna Lee Whitman and Michael Hayes, "Lou Pollak: The Road to Brown v. Board of Education and Beyond," *Proceedings of the American Philosophical Society* 158 (2014), 52; Clayborne Carson, "Two Cheers for Brown v. Board of Education," *Journal of American History* 91 (2004), 27–28; J. Michael McElreath, "The Cost of Opportunity: School Desegregation's Complicated Calculus in North Carolina," in *With All Deliberate Speed: Implementing Brown v. Board of Education*, ed. Brian J. Daugherity and Charles C. Bolton (University of Arkansas Press, 2008), 22, 24–25, 34–38; Frank Brown, "The First Serious Implementation of Brown: The 1964 Civil Rights Act and Beyond," *Journal of Negro Education* 50 (2004), 182, 186, 187, 188–189.

The Rev. Dr. Martin Luther King Jr. while doing a panel show called "Inside Black," to air on the ABC television network, in New York, June 30, 1963. Photograph by Allyn Baum/*The New York Times*/Redux.

20

Letter from the Birmingham Jail (1963)
Martin Luther King Jr

Introduction

"Letter from the Birmingham Jail" was written during a pivotal moment in the modern civil rights movement. Martin Luther King Jr., a Baptist minister from Georgia, became a prominent voice in the Black freedom movement of the mid-twentieth century, leading mass nonviolent protests against segregation, disfranchisement, and the economic marginalization of African Americans. From the Montgomery bus boycott of 1955–56 to the sit-in movement launched in 1960, King and others stirred the conscience of America like few social movements had before, demanding that the country live up to its democratic creed and Judeo-Christian values.

Despite some successes, opposition to the movement was both widespread and organized. By 1963, civil rights leaders believed that the cause needed a substantial and well-reported victory in a Deep South state—particularly one that seemed impervious to social change—in order to give it the momentum required to inspire additional societal support and to generate government intervention and meaningful federal legislation. After being tactically outmaneuvered by segregationist officials in Albany, Georgia, during protests in 1961–62, King and other leaders selected Birmingham, Alabama, as the site of the next major civil rights demonstrations. Birmingham, like Alabama more generally, had a long history of racial oppression and violence. In some circles, it had become known as "Bombingham," given the number of local Black churches that had been set ablaze by the Ku Klux Klan and other terrorist groups. Civil rights leaders believed that if segregation, employment discrimination, and other forms of racial discrimination could be publicly and successfully challenged in Birmingham, these markers of second-class citizenship could be contested any and everywhere.

Major civil rights protests of this period tended to follow a strategic and tactical script. Local leaders would identify problems that they hoped to resolve through protests, including marches, sit-ins, or boycotts. National figures such as King would then be invited to join the protests in order to heighten media coverage and to underscore the stakes involved. Televised acts of civil disobedience would test segregationist policies and other racially discriminatory statutes for the expressed purpose of triggering a response from local authorities. In many instances, the strategy worked like clockwork, and an outraged public, repulsed by violence directed toward peaceful demonstrators, would pressure mortified officials to address racial inequities.

In the case of Birmingham, a violent response to nonviolent protests was predictable. Unlike Albany officials, the local police chief, Eugene "Bull" Connor, did not seem to care that images of his deputies brutalizing protesters with billy clubs and police dogs were being broadcast around the world. King, who had been called in by local Black leaders to bolster their demands for desegregated public facilities and an end to job discrimination, was arrested during the protests and detained in the Birmingham Jail. In this heightened moment of tension and crisis, the civil rights leader was publicly criticized, notably by other clergy members, for leading protests against the established social order. In response to detractors, he penned a letter that would become foundational to the guiding ethos of the civil rights movement and its place in America's ongoing experiment in democratic government.—Claude A. Clegg

We were unable to obtain permission from the Estate of Martin Luther King Jr. in time to include it in this book. If you are a UNC at Chapel Hill student, the letter is available digitally through the University of North Carolina Libraries. Please visit www.uncpress.org/FAD-student-resources for a link to access the text through the library.

If you are a student that does not have access to the University of North Carolina Libraries, we recommend that you ask your professor or your institution's library if they can provide you with a copy. We will be updating www.uncpress.org/FAD-student-resources with information about other UNC System institutions who are able to provide their students with access to this text.

There are also numerous copies of the letter freely available online as scans or facsimiles of the original draft typed from Dr. King's hand-written notes.

Questions for Discussion

1. According to King, what are the four basic steps of a nonviolent campaign for social change? What are the purpose and goal of the "creative tension" that civil disobedience seeks to engender?
2. In the letter, what distinction does King make between a just law versus an unjust law? Why, according to King, would people be justified in defying an unjust law?
3. What is the basis of King's critique of white moderates? Why is he critical of the response of some white churches and clergy to the goals of the Black freedom movement?
4. How does King characterize the two opposing groups in the African American community that he and other leaders are appealing to and contending with? Which group do you think would have been most open to his leadership, cause, and methods? Which would be most resistant and why?
5. How does King's letter complement (or challenge) the arguments and conclusions of other historical documents—e.g., the U.S. Constitution or the Emancipation Proclamation—concerning the development, purpose, and meaning of American democracy and citizenship?

Further Reading

Carson, Clayborne, ed. *The Autobiography of Martin Luther King, Jr.* Warner Books, 1998.
Civil Rights Act. 1964. https://www.archives.gov/milestone-documents/civil-rights-act
King, Martin Luther, Jr. *Why We Can't Wait*. Mentor, 1964.
Vecchione, Judith, dir. *Eyes on the Prize: America's Civil Rights Movement*. 1987. Blackside, Inc.
Washington, James M., ed. *A Testament of Hope: The Essential Writings and Speeches of Martin Luther King, Jr.* Harper Collins, 1986.

Individuals march from the Governor's mansion to the capitol to support the Equal Rights Amendment – Tallahassee Florida. (1975, Donn Dughi.). Far left in the sunglasses is Rep. Karen Coolman, D-Ft. Lauderdale, then Rep. Gwen Cherry, D-Miami, at far right is Rep. Elaine Gordon. (Dughi, Donn, 1932–2005, Florida Memory: State Library and Archives of Florida)

21

Equal Rights Amendment (1972)
Alice Paul and Crystal Eastman

Introduction

For most of American history, sex equality was a radical idea. Women had no rights at the nation's founding: voting, entering contracts, owning property, and declining sex with their husbands were all off-limits to them. The nation's laws presumed that women did not need individual rights because they would marry, and their husbands' rights would protect them too. Women in the nineteenth century did occasionally demand fuller inclusion in the nation's civic life, but even some suffragists had pursued women's voting rights by framing their sex as society's moral housekeepers.

When the Nineteenth Amendment was ratified in 1920, opening the vote to millions of women, some women's advocates viewed full constitutional equality as the next step in their struggle. Two suffragists, Crystal Eastman and Alice Paul, drafted the Equal Rights Amendment (ERA) in 1923. They believed the ERA would remove the remaining impediments to women's citizenship, and, by extension, free members of their sex to define their own lives. But theirs was a minority position. Many women viewed the ERA as too broad and far-reaching. As evidence, some ERA opponents pointed to the sex-specific state laws that protected certain women from abuses in their jobs.

The ERA's momentum grew slowly at first, its text slightly altered from Eastman and Paul's, with members of Congress dutifully introducing it in each session. The amendment's prospects brightened in the late 1960s when a burgeoning feminist movement gave it a groundswell of energy. When an influx of women lawmakers centered the ERA as a legislative priority, both Houses of Congress approved it with vast bipartisan support by 1972. For the amendment to be added to the Constitution, thirty-eight state legislatures would need to follow suit within seven years. When thirty states ratified the ERA in the first year, its success seemed assured.

By the mid-1970s, ERA advocates had reason to worry. While they framed the ERA as the next piece of necessary work to perfect American democracy, a fusion of political and religious conservatives distilled concerns about changing gender roles into an anti-ERA movement. A new organization called STOP ERA, led by activist Phyllis Schlafly, claimed the ERA would breed disorder by making the sexes interchangeable: eroding nuclear families while ushering in same-sex marriage, women in combat, and gender-neutral restrooms. STOP ERA did help stop the ERA's progress. Congress extended the ratification timeline to give advocates three more years, but the ERA reached that 1982 deadline three states short.

In the decades since, courts and legislatures accomplished many of ERA advocates' original aims, and many of the consequences predicted by opponents of the amendment have also come to pass. But sex-based inequalities persist through gendered violence, economic disparities, and women's less-than-equal representation in politics. A broad coalition led by women of color and LGBTQ people has continued to push the ERA. Although three more state legislatures have ratified it, and President Joseph R. Biden declared it to be "the law of the land" in 2025, the ERA remains in limbo, saddled with legal and procedural ambiguities.—Katherine Turk

Section 1. Equality of rights under the law shall not be denied or abridged by the United States or by any state on account of sex.

Section 2. The Congress shall have the power to enforce, by appropriate legislation, the provisions of this article.

Section 3. This amendment shall take effect two years after the date of ratification.

Questions for Discussion

1. Why do you think the authors of the Equal Rights Amendment kept its main text so concise, at just twenty-four words?
2. How have the claims of advocates and opponents of the Equal Rights Amendment changed over time?
3. What do those changes in the claims of advocates and opponents reveal about shifts in Americans' notions of gender, rights, and family?

4. Why do you think the Equal Rights Amendment has been, and remains, so controversial—even among women? Why has sex equality been more divisive than other forms of equality described in this reader?
5. Considering the example of the Equal Rights Amendment, should we understand the process of amending the Constitution to be overly burdensome or an important check on popular whims?

Further Reading

Chisholm, Shirley. "Equal Rights for Women," Speech, Washington, DC, May 21, 1969.

Eastman, Crystal. "Now We Can Begin," *The Liberator*, December 1920.

Heckler, Margaret M., and Phyllis Schlafly, "Should the ERA Deadline be Extended?, Yes, No," *Christian Science Monitor*, February 7, 1978, 27.

Hill, Elsie Hill, and Florence Kelley. "Shall Women Be Equal Before the Law?," *The Nation*, April 12, 1922.

Pressley, Ayanna. "Pressley, Bush Launch First-Ever Congressional Equal Rights Amendment Caucus," Press release, March 28, 2023.

Contributors

W. Fitzhugh Brundage is the William B. Umstead Professor of History at the University of North Carolina at Chapel Hill. He studies American history since the Civil War with a particular focus on the American South. His works include *Lynching in the New South: Georgia and Virginia, 1880-1930* (1993), *The Southern Past: A Clash of Race and Memory* (2005), and *Civilizing Torture: An American Tradition* (2018).

Claude A. Clegg teaches African American and U.S. history at the University of North Carolina at Chapel Hill. He is the author of several books, including *The Black President: Hope and Fury in the Age of Obama* and *An Original Man: The Life and Times of Elijah Muhammad*.

Kathleen DuVal is the Carl W. Ernst Distinguished Professor of History at the University of North Carolina at Chapel Hill. She studies early America, particularly how various Native American, European, and African women and men interacted from the sixteenth through early nineteenth centuries. Her books include *Native Nations: A Millennium in North America* (2024) and *Independence Lost: Lives on the Edge of the American Revolution* (2015).

Raquel Escobar is an assistant professor of history at the University of North Carolina at Chapel Hill. Escobar specializes in twentieth-century histories of race and Indigeneity in the United States.

Erik S. Gellman is a professor of history at the University of North Carolina at Chapel Hill. His books include *Death Blow to Jim Crow: The National Negro Congress and the Rise of Militant Civil Rights* (2012) and *Troublemakers: Chicago Freedom Struggles through the Lens of Art Shay* (2020).

Joseph T. Glatthaar is the Stephenson Distinguished Professor of History at the University of North Carolina at Chapel Hill. He studies the American Civil War and American military history. His works include *American Military History: A Very Short Introduction* (2020) and *General Lee's Army: From Victory to Collapse* (2008).

Sophia Howells is the administrative support associate in the Department of History at the University of North Carolina at Chapel Hill and earned her Bachelor's degree in Global Studies from Carolina in 2012.

Antwain K. Hunter is an assistant professor of history at the University of North Carolina at Chapel Hill. He studies slavery and freedom in North America, with a current focus on the Carolinas. His book, *A Precarious Balance: Firearms, Race, and Community in North Carolina, 1729-1865*, will be published in Fall 2025. Hunter has previously published the Springfield Armory in the *North Carolina Historical Review*, the *Journal of Family History*, and the *Journal of Military History*.

Miguel La Serna is the chair of the Department of History at the University of North Carolina at Chapel Hill and a Bowman & Gordon Gray Distinguished Term Professor of History. His books include *With Masses and Arms: Peru's Tupac Amaru Revolutionary Movement* (2020) and *The Shining Path: Love, Madness, and Revolution in the Andes* (co-authored with Orin Starn 2019).

Heather Ruth Lee is an assistant professor of history at the University of North Carolina at Chapel Hill. She specializes in U.S. immigration history during the nineteenth and twentieth centuries, with an emphasis on the intersection between immigration law and business strategies. Her first book, *Gastrodiplomacy: Chinese Exclusion and the Ascent of Chinese Restaurants in New York*, will be published by the University of Chicago Press in 2026.

Katherine Turk is a professor of history and an adjunct professor of women's and gender studies at the University of North Carolina at Chapel Hill. Her books include *Equality on Trial: Gender and Rights in the Modern American Workplace* (2016) and *The Women of NOW: How Feminists Built an Organization that Transformed America* (2023).

Molly Worthen is a professor of history at the University of North Carolina at Chapel Hill. She studies North American religious and intellectual history. Her works include *Spellbound: How Charisma Shaped American History from the Puritans to Donald Trump* (2025), *Apostles of Reason: The Crisis of Authority in American Evangelicalism* (2013) and *The Man on Whom Nothing Was Lost: The Grand Strategy of Charles Hill* (2006).